"From the heart of one who personally understands the pain of infertility, Dr. Meaney has provided a truly invaluable resource for all who experience this pain and for the friends and family members who want to console and accompany them. Through sharing the lessons learned from her own experience, Dr. Meaney helps couples experiencing infertility to better understand and respond to the suffering that accompanies it and to find real hope and inner peace from the infinite love of God and the loving guidance and practical help he provides through his Church."

ARCHBISHOP JOSEPH F. NAUMANN
Archbishop of Kansas City in Kansas

"Dr. Marie Meaney has created a compelling masterpiece! She brilliantly combines her personal challenges with infertility and a robust bioethical assessment of reproductive technologies. This richly detailed book sheds light on sensitive moral issues while presenting the complex web of risks, consequences, morbidities, and promising hopes that surround the struggle to balance core values which recognize the embryo as a living being who deserves our sacred reverence. The result is a profound, understandable, well-researched, and practical guide that is a must-have for anyone suffering from infertility—and for their pastors, counselors, and loved ones. This book is convincing, compassionate, and comprehensibly Catholic!"

THERESA BURKE
Founder of Rachel's Vineyard Ministries and author of
Forbidden Grief: The Unsp̶̶

"Salvation history is the story of God's faithful accompaniment of his people through their pain and suffering and the transformation that is possible when we surrender to his divine providence and tender care. Dr. Marie Meaney beautifully expresses this understanding in *When Expecting Doesn't Happen,* saying 'The cross [of infertility] is tremendously heavy, if we carry it on our own.' However, 'Christ promises that it will become light if we carry it with him.'

I have seen the emotional devastation that infertility can cause to couples and the grave harm caused from an erroneous conscience regarding Catholic teaching on assisted reproductive technologies. This book will not only assist married couples, but it will also greatly benefit friends, families, pastors, catechists, physicians, and family counselors. I highly recommend this book."

FR. SHENAN J. BOUQUET
President of Human Life International

"This is more than a book about the pain of infertility. It is a friend to those who are on this journey; it is a trove of wisdom and compassion. In short, it is a gift. Meaney explores the wounds of infertility and guides the reader, with gentleness and clarity, through the moral labyrinth of potential treatments. Meaney is more than a Catholic ethicist, however. She is someone who has been on the journey herself and whose faith is exemplary. Her writing on suffering stands out as luminous spiritual guidance, whatever the reader's wound. The book also contains sections aimed at family and friends of the infertile couple detailing how best to help and understand the situation. This is a rare thing: a useful and beautiful book."

SALLY READ
Poet and author of Night's Bright Darkness:
A Modern Conversion Story

"All women are mothers: either physically, spiritually, or both. All mothers create. What happens, though, when that act of creation only lives in a mother's desires, best hopes, and open heart? Dr. Marie Meaney faithfully explains how to respond to the 'royal road of the cross' of infertility. For all who struggle with infertility: let Dr. Meaney's wisdom inspire you to always see the grace and goodness of our gracious and good God."

BARBARA MCGUIGAN
Host of "Fight for Life" on Virgin Most Powerful Radio

"Engagingly presented in a narrative built upon Dr. Meaney's own experience with infertility, this little book is a goldmine of spiritual, emotional, and bioethical information and practical counsel on the topic. The author's generous use of quotes from the saints, important passages from Church documents, and real-life stories of struggle and victory makes the text fresh and appealing, and the personal witness testimonies that are included bring to life the studies cited in support of the Church's teaching on reproductive technology. Throughout the work, Dr. Meaney demonstrates a deep understanding of the Catholic view of the human person and the call to genuine love, great insight into the formative power and redemptive value of suffering, and a wonderful compassion enabling her to speak to the heart."

MARIA FEDORYKA
Associate Professor of Philosophy at Ave Maria University and author of The Special Gift of Woman

"*When Expecting Doesn't Happen* is a unique and invaluable resource for any couple suffering from infertility, including secondary infertility (wanting more children but being unable to conceive), and for those around the couple who are unsure what to say or do. The book is filled with practical help: from how to handle a baby shower invitation to finding medical help that can bring healing (and potentially conception) rather than harm. The book is a must-read for every person in the pro-life movement because of its sensitivity to the infertility often suffered by women who have had abortions and also for its discussion of common infertility treatments. Most pro-lifers have little to no understanding of in-vitro fertilization (IVF), its connection to abortion, and its disregard for the dignity of the person. Meaney's discussion is disturbing, moving, and powerfully persuasive."

PEGGY HARTSHORN
Board Chair of Heartbeat International

When

EXPECTING

Doesn't Happen

When
EXPECTING
Doesn't Happen

Turning Infertility into a
JOURNEY OF HOPE

MARIE MEANEY, D.PHIL.

EMMAUS
ROAD
PUBLISHING
Steubenville, Ohio
www.emmausroad.org

Emmaus Road Publishing
1468 Parkview Circle
Steubenville, Ohio 43952

Library of Congress Control Number 9781645852100
ISBN 978-1-64585-210-0 paperback | 978-1-64585-211-7 ebook

Cover design and original artwork by Patty Borgman
Layout by Allison Merrick

For Joseph

CONTENTS

FOREWORD

The pain and struggles of infertility are *real*. We've experienced them firsthand.

When we married at age twenty-four, we were in blissful, naïve love. We married in the Catholic Church yet began our marriage using the birth control pill. We were unaware of Church teachings on contraception and felt that we wanted to be "in control" of our lives and childbearing. Upon deciding that *we* were ready to have children, we got off the pill . . . and were in for a rude awakening. Within short order, we realized that something was wrong: We were unable to conceive. Month after month, year after year, we could not achieve a pregnancy.

Friends and family members were getting pregnant, which became increasingly painful. Through these years, we spent much time on our knees in prayer and grew closer to God. We investigated medical options for couples experiencing infertility but were horrified by what we found: inhumane reproductive procedures and technologies that conflicted with our faith and contradicted our pro-life efforts.

Amidst this season of searching and suffering, we were asked to speak at a Pre-Cana marriage preparation workshop. During that event, we heard—for the first time—a presentation about the profound wisdom of St. Paul VI's encyclical, *Humanae Vitae*. We learned how natural fertility methods can be utilized if there are well-grounded reasons for spacing births, and we were stunned to discover that these methods can provide help in achieving pregnancy, even for those experiencing infertility. We were hooked.

We began using Dr. Thomas Hilgers' NaPro Technology methods to assess what was going on. It quickly became clear that Margaret was experiencing polycystic ovarian disease and endometriosis and that medical intervention would be necessary. The Natural Family Planning coordinator for our diocese explained that the procedures would be costly—possibly as expensive as a car—and likely would not be covered by our health insurance. But he asked us: "Which do you value more: a new car or the possibility of having a child?" The answer was clear to us.

We invested the time and money to travel to the Saint Paul VI Institute in Omaha, Nebraska, where Dr. Hilgers performed laparoscopic surgery on Margaret. At the end, he said, "I think you will be able to get pregnant, but I can't guarantee it. If you aren't pregnant in eighteen months, come back here and we'll assess next steps."

We went home with a glimmer of hope . . . and thirty days later, Margaret was pregnant.

For the next nine months, things were not easy. The pregnancy was high risk and Margaret had to endure painful weekly progesterone shots, regular blood draws, and screening tests to preserve the life of our first child. After a life-threatening scare caused by placenta previa, our daughter Claire was born through an emergency C-section. We sent her baby photo to Dr. Hilgers, and it was posted on the Saint Paul VI Institute "miracle baby" wall.

We next experienced a heartbreaking miscarriage before Dr. Hilgers was able to help us achieve one more pregnancy, albeit high risk. Nine more months of painful progesterone shots, blood draws, and tests. But at the end, our son Patrick was born. Another photo was posted on Dr. Hilgers' wall. And miraculously, our health insurance covered the costs.

We were never able to conceive again but are eternally thankful for the gift of our children. Today, our daughter is Sr. Gloria Christi, a Nashville Dominican sister. Our son, Patrick, studies Global Affairs at George Mason University and is a leader in the Catholic Campus Ministry and pro-life efforts on campus.

We recognize that not every infertility story has the same ending as ours. Some couples who experience the pain and struggles of infertility are never able to have children and carry this burden for a lifetime. Reflecting on our experiences, and those of others who have grappled with infertility and experienced different outcomes, we are so thankful for Marie Meaney's beautiful book, *When Expecting Doesn't Happen: Turning Infertility into a Journey of Hope.* This is the resource we wish we'd had amidst our infertility difficulties, and you now hold it in your hands.

Marie brilliantly tackles the topic of infertility in a thorough, practical, and accessible way. She brings science, lived experience, and Catholic teaching to bear while addressing this difficult topic in a readable, compassionate way. Throughout this book, Marie comes alongside you as a trusted, understanding guide.

Marie is the real deal. We've known the Meaney family for many years and have been on similar paths. Margaret grew up with Marie's husband, Joseph, in Corpus Christi, and they attended the same parish. Both of our families have struggled with infertility challenges while involved in full-time ministry work. In our case, David led a local pro-life organization before eventually founding and leading the global 40 Days for Life movement through its first decade while Margaret was homeschooling our children. We've admired the Meaney's ministry work from a distance as they've moved around the world serving Christ and His Church.

Marie's heart for God and love of others radiates throughout this book. Whether you are personally suffering from the pain and anguish of infertility or have a family member or friend who is, you will benefit from Marie's wisdom and consolation within the pages of *When Expecting Doesn't Happen*. As a couple that has personally experienced infertility challenges, we wholeheartedly endorse this book and know that it will provide perspective, peace, and comfort for a whole new generation.

David and Margaret Bereit

PREFACE

When I originally wrote about infertility in 2006, my husband and I had been married for six years and were still childless. It would take another three years before we would be blessed with our little Thérèse—on the feast of the archangels in 2009. Since then, I have reworked this text multiple times, and it has appeared in book form in English, Spanish, German, Croatian, Hungarian, and French.[1] I expanded the French version by two-thirds, and it is in light of the latter edition that I have rewritten the book in English.

During these difficult nine years, we understood and accepted the Church's teaching on *in vitro* fertilization (IVF) as a law of life, but we didn't know how to live with the excruciatingly painful absence of children on a daily basis. Neither was it easy to know how to speak with our friends and family about it, nor how to deal

---

[1] Here is a list of the various earlier and much shorter editions: English: *Embracing the Cross of Infertility* (Front Royal, VA: HLI, 2006), CD-ROM; 2010, booklet; Spanish: *Aceptación de la Cruz de la Infertilidad*, trans. Elizabeth Irigoyen (Front Royal, VA: HLI, 2011); Hungarian: *A meddőség kdaeresztje*, ed. Imre Téglásy and Judit Szigeti-Ferenczy, trans. Istvánfi Gáborné (Budapest: Nyomda, 2011); German: *Das Kreuz der Unfruchtbarkeit* (Salzburg: Immaculata Verlag, 2012); Croatian *Prihvatiti križ neplodnosti* (Zagreb: Nonnatus, 2012); and French, in a longer edition: *Une grossesse tant désirée* (Paris: Téqui, 2016).

with hurtful comments and clumsy attempts to give us advice. This book attempts to help couples suffering from infertility to grapple with these difficulties in a more fruitful way, hopefully lessening some of their burdens and turning this human tragedy into a journey of hope and growth.

By presenting our questions and reflections, our lessons learned of how to deal better with this burden during the seemingly endless waiting time, I would like to share our own journey and experience. The six chapters of this book try to address different facets of the issue.

The first chapter describes the experience of infertility for those unfamiliar with it and to give some stats to show the sheer magnitude of the problem. When I speak of "infertile couples" for the sake of brevity, it is important to forebear from defining them as such, as if infertility were at the heart of their marriage. I am using the term in its strictly biological sense, for childless couples can, of course, be fruitful in many other ways through their gift of self to others. And conversely, a couple with children can still be spiritually sterile, if they are, for example, selfish or abusive.

The second section speaks of the spiritual and psychological traps into which we infertile couples are tempted to fall. Had I been told that certain well-intentioned attitudes and decisions would be dead ends, I would have dealt with this suffering much better. Instead of straining to hold it all together, for example, which seemed courageous and virtuous at the time, I would have done well to let go, allow myself to grieve, and start with the actual mourning process.

The third chapter attempts to help those surrounding the couple in question. Family members and friends often feel helpless and don't know what to do or say. It can be difficult for them to understand what makes this desire for children so heart-wrenching. And the spouses, feeling very raw inside, frequently find themselves incapable of articulating why this experience is so painful. That is why I kept this book short; it can be quickly perused and specific chapters that are relevant to some situations read separately for guidance.

The excruciatingly painful desire of those suffering from infertility drives them to make use of reproductive technologies that will—so they hope—give them the long-expected child or children. I understand that pain and desire from the inside, but some of these technologies go against love itself, since they contradict the human dignity of the child and of the couple. That is why they are forbidden by the Catholic Church. They oppose some fundamental laws of life, leaving potentially profound wounds in the people affected. I attempt to show the philosophical and theological reasonings against Artificial Reproductive Technologies (ART) in chapter four and offer much more promising alternatives in chapter five.

Finally, in the last chapter, I try to give some spiritual advice and some pointers as to how to continue the journey with hope and inner peace.

I end with a personal postscript, tying up some loose ends and giving some final advice. The book concludes with a few essays on topics related to the issue.

Our story has a beautiful conclusion, but this should not give the false impression that we are now speaking from the blissful heights of parenting while handing down meager crumbs of advice to those who still feel crushed by their childlessness. Yes, it is true that having a child makes a universe of a difference compared to having none. However, the pain of secondary infertility (when one has already one or several children but would like more) is also very great. We suffered from it for many years after a heartbreaking miscarriage in 2011, fearing that more children would not come easily to us, and we have now passed the age of childbearing. Hence, we too are still on this journey, trying to come to terms with the fact that we don't have a house full of children as we would have liked, yet realizing that we can nonetheless have a rich life, as we have been very blessed with our daughter.

I would like to thank my husband, Joseph, who encouraged me to write this book and with whom I have carried the cross of infertility for many years. This experience has brought us closer together, and we love each other more deeply and better as a result. I also wish to thank our friends and family members who consoled us and helped us discreetly, giving us the space to mourn. What would I have done without my friend, Maria Fedoryka, who embodies the Christian virtue of compassion like no one else and has been an incredible support on this journey! My parents have been of great assistance, while others have helped us by keeping a discreet but supportive distance.

My thoughts and prayers go out to those with whom we have shared this plight, whose courage has inspired us and whose sadness we have tried to shoulder with them. Our gratitude toward the Catholic Church, our mother, is infinite, for she guided us and protected us against choices that would have been very hurtful to us and others.

Chapter 1

EXPERIENCING INFERTILITY

I t seems like the world is standing on its head. On the one hand, some want free and legal access to abortion during the nine months of pregnancy, while others are struggling with infertility. God is giving children to those who don't want them, and not to those who would be loving parents—at least, so it often seems to those suffering from infertility who wonder why.

We are so steeped in the culture of death, having made ourselves the masters over life and death, that we think babies will come along when it suits our plans. This mentality can even affect those who are pro-life and recognize each child as a special gift of God. To the cross of infertility that has existed since time immemorial is now added the temptation of a quasi-omnipotence, of having children no matter what it takes, even if it means manufacturing them and killing some in the process.

SOME STATS

Though infertility has obviously always existed as we can see from the stories of Sarah, Hannah, or Elizabeth, who eventually became the mothers of Isaac and the prophets Samuel and St. John the Baptist respectively, in the Old and New Testaments, it never seems to have been so widespread. At least 80 million people suffer from infertility, according to a World Health Organization (WHO) Report from 2002, which was confirmed in 2010, when the WHO re-studied the question; infertility had stayed about the same from 1990 to 2010, which comes down to one in four couples suffering from infertility within the developing world.[1] According to the study, 1.9% of women between the ages of twenty and forty-four who wanted a child were unable to have their first living baby, while 10.5% of women who had previously given birth were unable to have another baby after trying for five years.[2] In the US, 6.7 million women between the ages of

---

[1] World Health Organization (WHO), *Current Practices and Controversies in Assisted Reproduction: Report of a Meeting on "Medical, Ethical and Social Aspects of Assisted Reproduction" Held at WHO Headquarters in Geneva, Switzerland 17–21 September 2001*, ed. Effy Vayena, Patrick J. Rowe, P. David Griffin (Geneva: WHO, 2002), p. xv, http://www.who.int/reproduc tivehealth/publications/infertility/9241590300/en; "Global Prevalence of Infertility, Infecundity, and Childlessness," WHO, accessed July 1, 2020, http://www.who.int/reproductivehealth/topics/infertility/burden/en/in dex.html; see the report Maya N. Mascarenhas et al., "National, Regional, and Global Trends in Infertility Prevalence since 1990: A Systematic Analysis of 277 Health Surveys," PLOS Medicine, PLOS, December 18, 2012, doi.org/10.1371/journal.pmed.1001356; according to the report from Shea O. Rutstein and Iqbal H. Shah, *DHS Comparative Reports 9: Infecundity, Infertility, and Childlessness in Developing Countries* (Calverton, MD: ORC Macro and WHO, 2004), https://www.who.int/reproductivehealth/topics /infertility/DHS-CR9.pdf, in the developing world the numbers are quite high: "Seventeen percent of women age 15 to 49 report themselves as infecund," p. xiii.

[2] Dr. Charlotte Warren-Gash, "Worldwide Infertility Rates Unchanged in

fifteen and forty-four are suffering from an impaired ability to have children, which is 10.9% of women in that age range; 8.8% of married women are suffering from infertility, while 12% have impaired fecundity regardless of their marital status, according to the statistics of the Centers for Disease Control and Prevention.[3] Infertility does not only affect those who have no children, but also those who have started a family. Secondary infertility (after the birth of one or more children) is a common phenomenon and can be a hidden suffering.

A couple is medically defined as being infertile if they are not using contraception and yet have not been able to conceive over a period of twelve months or more. According to the Mayo Clinic, this is due in one-third of all cases to male infertility, in another one-third of cases to female infertility, and for the remainder it is a combination of factors in both, with 20% of the cases remaining unexplained.[4]

REASONS FOR INFERTILITY

The reasons for infertility are varied. For the woman, it can be the failure to ovulate, blocked fallopian tubes, hormonal imbalance, endometriosis, or polycystic ovarian syndrome, among other

20 Years Says World Health Organisation," BioNews, Progress Educational Trust, January 7, 2013, http://www.bionews.org.uk/page_232839.asp.

[3] "Infertility," National Center for Health Statistics, Centers for Disease Control and Prevention (CDC), accessed October 7, 2020, http://www.cdc.gov/nchs/fastats/infertility.htm. These data are valid for 2015–2017; "Infertility FAQs," National Center for Chronic Disease Prevention and Health Promotion, CDC, accessed October 7, 2020, https://www.cdc.gov/reproductivehealth/infertility/index.html.

[4] "Infertility," Mayo Clinic, accessed February 26, 2021, https://www.mayoclinic.org/diseases-conditions/infertility/symptoms-causes/syc-20354317.

things.[5] For the man, it can be a low sperm count (oligospermia), sperm which lacks motility or has a high percentage of abnormal morphology, or even a complete lack of sperm (azoospermia). Men's sperm levels and quality seem to be progressively going down. In 2017, for example, researchers from the Hebrew University and Mount Sinai's medical school found that sperm counts per milliliter of semen had decreased by more than 50% from 1973 to 2011 in a survey of nearly 43,000 men from North America, Europe, New Zealand, and Australia.[6]

Birth control can be another factor, for it often affects hormones over long periods, even after its discontinued use.[7] What its effects are over future generations remains to be seen. This as well as the stress of modern life, poor nutrition and sleeping habits, environmental factors, and other factors can affect a couple's fertility.

---

[5] Furthermore, previous abortions may have scarred the uterus or damaged the cervix, making implantation or the carrying to term of the pregnancy difficult.

[6] Ashley Fetters, "Sperm Counts Continue to Fall," *The Atlantic*, October 12, 2018, https://www.theatlantic.com/family/archive/2018/10/sperm-counts-continue-to-fall/572794/.

[7] Fearing that the hormones from the Pill could eventually get into the drinking-water, Japan had prohibited its use until 1999. In some rivers the percentage of hormones is so high, that the fish change their sex. In an article from January 20, 2009, in UK Research and Innovation, NERC, "River Sewage Pollution Found to be Disrupting Fish Hormones," the author, Tom Marshall, describes this phenomenon in the U.K., suggesting that it might be the reason for the increase of infertility among human beings. http://planet earth.nerc.ac.uk/news/story.aspx?id=297. In an article "Why Are These Male Fish Growing Eggs?," published in the *National Geographic* on February 3, 2016, Lindsey Konkel points out that even in wildlife refuges, a high percentage of male fish grow eggs in testes; in 19 such refuges in the United States and in Northern Europe, 60%–100% of male small mouth bass were doing so. Which endocrine-disrupting chemicals produce this change is not yet clear, though the Pill is high on the list of suspects. https://www.national geographic.com/news/2016/02/160203-feminized-fish-endocrine-disrup tion-hormones-wildlife-refuges/#close.

The problem of infertility is furthermore aggravated, since people marry ever later on average, given the cultural context. While some simply don't meet their spouse until their thirties or later, others want to complete their studies and be well established professionally before having a child. In the United States, 20% wait until the age of thirty-five before trying to bear children, which shows how much the culture has changed over the last fifty years.[8] The average age of a woman having her first child went from twenty-one years old in 1972 to twenty-six years old in 2016. As the stats show, in society at large an important factor in delaying childbirth is education. A woman with a college degree living in a big city will on average postpone having children by about seven years—not because education as such is at fault, but because of the societal values attached to professional success after having spent time and money on a university. In New York, for example, that woman will be thirty-one years old, while in Zapata County in Texas, she will be twenty-one[9]

Infertility can have significant psychological repercussions, leading sometimes to depression, and, in any case, to great sorrow. Already Rachel cried to her husband Jacob in the book of Genesis: "Give me children, or I shall die!" (Gen 30:1).[10] This cry of anguish

---

[8] This was mentioned in the original report of the American Society for Reproductive Medicine (ASRM), *Age and Fertility: A Guide for Parents* (Birmingham, AL: ASRM), 2003, https://fwivf.com/new-patient/docu ments/AgeandFertilityGuide.pdf, p. 3. Its revised version from 2012 simply mentions that women often wait until their thirties to try to have children (Birmingham, AL: ASRM, 2012), https://www.reproductivefacts.org/global assets/rf/news-and-publications/bookletsfact-sheets/english-fact-sheets-and -info-booklets/Age_and_Fertility.pdf.

[9] Quoctrung Bui and Claire Cain Miller, "The Age that Women Have Babies: How a Gap Divides America," *The New York Times*, August 4, 2018, https:// www.nytimes.com/interactive/2018/08/04/upshot/up-birth-age-gap.html.

[10] *Catechism of the Catholic Church*, 2nd ed. (Washington, DC: Libreria

shows how infertility affects the woman in a particular way, though it can also be very painful for her husband (indeed, sometimes the husband suffers from the childlessness more than his wife). She is the one who physically experiences pregnancy, feeling the child grow in her womb, as St. John Paul II said so beautifully in *Mulieris Dignitatem*, and thus she will probably feel more deeply their absence.[11]

However, we should not forget that not only couples have to grapple with childlessness. Single people also, if they know they are sterile, or simply don't find a spouse, have to bear this cross. Single women who are getting older must face the possibility of never having children of their own. As they age, their panic and their sorrow can grow. Their suffering does not end once they are past menopause.

This book is primarily geared toward couples experiencing infertility and their families, although some things I say might also be helpful to singles. For the latter, to the pain of not finding a spouse is added the ache of not having children, with the biological clock ticking increasingly louder for women as they approach the climacteric.

For those who have not experienced infertility themselves, it can be quite difficult to imagine the nature of this suffering.

Editrice Vaticana–United States Conference of Catholic Bishops, 2000), § 2374 (hereafter cited in text as CCC).

[11] "Motherhood *is linked to the personal structure of the woman and to the personal dimension of the gift.*" Pope John Paul II, Apostolic Letter on the Dignity and Vocation of Women *Mulieris Dignitatem* (August 15, 1988), § 18, italics in original. I will therefore focus more on the woman's experience of infertility, which I obviously know from personal experience. However, much of what I write also applies to the man. For example, to get a man's perspective, see Shaun A. McAfee, "The Deep Pain of Infertility: A Man's Perspective," *Aleteia*, June 4, 2014, https://aleteia.org/2014/06/04/the-deep -pain-of-infertility-a-mans-perspective.

Though I had always felt very sorry for couples who could not conceive, I really did not have a clue what the experience was like before it happened to me. Having said this, people react to infertility in very diverse ways. Not everyone suffers deeply from it. Some—even if pro-life—experience little or no pain, while others are utterly crushed; again, others suffer without it putting their whole life into question.

WHAT IT MEANS TO EXPERIENCE INFERTILITY

What does it mean to suffer from infertility? It is difficult to explain. How can I render palpable this desire which relentlessly, inescapably wrenches the heart? I dream to come home to children welcoming me with excitement or even problems, a house filled with their cries and laughter.[12] Without children, I might even come to feel something lacking in my relationship to my spouse. Clearly, the love among infertile couples is not inferior, nor their marriages of lesser value. But since children are the fruit of the spouses' love for each other, their absence can be felt keenly. It is something extraordinary to become parents together, to see the other in his or her role as father or mother, to help each other to become better parents.

It is truly amazing that through the union of the husband and wife, by a superabundance of their love, a new human being sees the light of day. Love always generates more love, but here this

---

[12] This is not to negate the difficulties of parenting, nor that some go through a real Calvary with their children, ranging from terrible illness to death, discord, and estrangement. But children are a gift which one cannot bestow on oneself. Their absence can therefore be sorely felt, just like the single person's desire for a spouse does not disappear despite the knowledge that some marriages are unhappy.

love manifests itself in the creation of a new person. Of course, the spouses don't bring forth this child solely by their own powers. It always takes an act of God, who creates each individual soul and permits the parents to participate in this act by becoming procreators. As the mother of the seven martyrs beautifully says in the second book of Maccabees, "I do not know how you came into being in my womb. It was not I who gave you life and breath, nor I who set in order the elements within each of you" (2 Macc 7:22).

Though God is the source of human life and of every human soul, He generally bows down to the biological limitations of the spouses. Short of a miracle, as depicted in some of the stories in the Old Testament, a couple with certain medical conditions or beyond a certain age will not conceive children. They may long intensely for children, to the point of experiencing this suffering as heartbreak. Only a child, it seems, would fulfill this desire and make them happy. They want to become parents and participate in a new way in the great mystery of life, hopefully bringing future citizens of heaven into this world. They wish to work together in the great adventure of raising children. But infertility robs them of this possibility.

Infertility can mean, therefore, a complete change of my plan for life. Except if I know that I or my husband are sterile (sterility having a finality to it that infertility does not), there is hope and disappointment every month; and this disappointment comes at a time when it is emotionally and hormonally the most difficult for the woman. At some moments, her hopes rise, and it takes a pregnancy test before she realizes that she has hoped yet again in vain. Perhaps she has been able to conceive, yet has miscarried, which adds a new, terrible sorrow. Some women feel that their life is on hold during this time: they are simply waiting for children, and during this time, not much else makes sense. No profession, no successful career can fill the emptiness caused by infertility.

Common to all of this is a feeling of helplessness, a sense of our limitations. Perhaps we thought initially that infertility would never be an issue, that this kind of thing happens only to others. Thus, the realization that something is wrong hits us as a great shock. At first, we are under the impression that we will be able to overcome this problem with the help of doctors, inner resilience, and positive thinking. We hear about stories where people discovered their key issue and then, suddenly, the babies came in abundance. Yet, for some reason, this doesn't seem to be our own story. The waiting continues, the years pass, and mere human, natural hope starts to fail. We notice that our family and friends have given up hope, which depresses us further. We are confronted with our powerlessness at fixing the problem, while the sense of frustration and sadness only grows. "Why is God allowing this to happen?" we may be asking ourselves. "Why is it that others have no problems having babies?" We seem to be missing the secret of how to be fertile, trying to pull ourselves into a position of "positive thinking" and "no stress," from where conception and bringing a baby to term will be possible.

During my experience of infertility and that of other women I encountered, I have not only come to see what is common to this excruciatingly painful experience, but also what typically defines wrong attempts at resolving it. Barrenness is a terrible suffering, but it can be made ten times worse by adopting false solutions.

Thus, I will address in the next chapter the attitudes and choices that the couple would do better to avoid, however right they may seem at first.

Chapter 2

DEAD ENDS VERSUS
NEW BEGINNINGS

As couples start realizing that something isn't quite right and that babies aren't coming as easily as expected, they have to face many heartaches. The typical pattern of denial, anger, bargaining, and depression seem to be on a perpetual loop, while acceptance seems impossible. Once the couple is beyond denial and takes on a proactive attitude, they find themselves (except if their medical issue is easily solved) frustrated that nothing seems to be working. Promising medical treatments fail to give them the much-desired child, while positive thinking flounders very soon and the throbbing pain in their hearts only seems to be getting worse.

The temptation to adopt a wrong attitude or to take shortcuts is great. Sometimes we are even under the false impression that this is pleasing to God. It is normal to want to alleviate our suffering, and indeed we should do so. But it is important to realize that some methods make matters worse and embitter the heart.

Trying to Avoid Suffering at the Cost of Mourning

I wish to do the right thing, to carry my cross courageously, not wanting to burden others with my sorrow, and I therefore strive to control my emotions. Though courage and self-denial are admirable virtues, they can be problematic when they come at the cost of mourning. Then they grow into an avoidance mechanism. The implicit expectation is that somehow I can hoist myself out of my pain by holding it all together. But this, unfortunately, is rarely the case. Paradoxically, by trying to evade a suffering that I cannot resolve, I remain stuck in it. Instead, by accepting it, I can get beyond the acute sting and embittering hopelessness, eventually finding inner peace. But this is difficult, often long and heartbreakingly painful. And it means humbly accepting that I have to let go—though of course, I can and should continue to look for medical solutions.

Even if dealt with admirably, infertility remains a suffering for many. I cannot escape the pain, and if I try, I will never find true peace. By embracing the Cross, I will hopefully come to feel ultimately that its burden is light; if I shun it, it will crush me all the more. I am asked to make an act of trust rather than of courage, namely to recognize that God is greater than this abyss of pain which threatens to devour me. So, I need to ask myself: Have I truly allowed myself to experience fully the suffering of childlessness, or am I trying to escape from it by embracing a stoic attitude?

Also, I need to be aware that there are different stages of mourning and that I might well never be quite done, though it becomes easier. When menopause starts announcing itself or the woman has a hysterectomy, when the time comes that we should have become grandparents, we will have to face our infertility again. Invited to yet another baby shower or baptism, another announcement by a friend that she is pregnant, the pain might well resurface. We may have thought that we were past this stage of taxing grief and be surprised by its intensity. But mourning is a process; though the pain lessens, it still manifests itself at certain moments.

There is no pre-set pattern as to how long or at which moments these phases of mourning hit us; and there is no shortcut to grieving our infertility, even though we can find support, consolation, and ultimately inner peace (though that is a gift, and not something we can bestow on ourselves). We have to traverse this mourning before we can find the peace and serenity which God promised to those who follow Him (see John 14:27).

The Pitfalls of Self-pity

As with all protracted suffering, I can easily feel sorry for myself after a while. If I have experienced some other great sufferings in my life, it is tempting to feel singled out by destiny as its permanent victim. It is not enough to pull myself together, for that is just a Band-Aid on this festering wound that has deeper, spiritual roots. The self-pity will still be present, though it may hide as aggression or lead to depression, and I will have pushed myself even further away from being able to resolve what is slowly poisoning my soul.

So what can I do about self-pity when it hits me? I can thank God for the good things He has given me (which does not mean denying the reality of this pain) and focus on His love as a father to counter the pull of self-pity. And again, I can truly grieve the absence of children. Otherwise, I cannot help but drag this pain around, whatever I do and wherever I go, feeling continuously crushed by something I cannot shake off, that I cannot run away from, and which remains external since I haven't accepted it. Paradoxically, it is by going through the mourning process by many small acts of trust in God that I will ultimately be able to accept this pain and avoid the resentment which lurks at the heart of self-pity.

Couples suffering from infertility shouldn't be hard on themselves either. It is normal to feel sorry for ourselves in such circumstances, and it is good to see this feeling as an invitation to grieve.[1] Let us have a bit of compassion on ourselves, give ourselves some space, and allow for the emotions that arise!

Even if we cannot help but feel self-pity now and then, we can at least try to avoid becoming passive as a consequence. An acquaintance of mine who had suffered from infertility for six years tried a medical procedure from which she had expected much; but when she did not conceive soon thereafter, she felt so sorry for herself that she did not want to follow up. Happily, her husband convinced her otherwise, for she now has a little girl. Had she given way to discouragement that little girl would not exist today.

Getting Diagnosis and Treatment

It seems obvious, but trying to find out the reasons for one's infertility and then addressing them is essential. Denial is, after all, a very common first reaction. But when it lasts longer, it becomes

---

[1]   Also, self-pity may be an indication that there are other areas in our life, other sufferings, which we haven't yet "suffered through," haven't fully accepted yet, and which need to be revisited in the light of God's love for us.

a real problem. Having to face the painful reality of infertility is hard, but at the same time it is the only way to start resolving it.

People who are very abandoned to God's will might not take any initiative, thinking that God will simply resolve the problem. Yes, He might, but He also wants us to use the (licit) medical tools available for healing. After all, if I have appendicitis I won't refuse to see a doctor because I believe that God will heal me! If I did, this would not merely be foolish but also a sin against my body, which is a gift from God.

However, each couple has to decide what methods of diagnosis and treatment make sense for them given their financial situation, opportunities, and geographical location. But I would suggest thinking creatively and keeping an open mind about available ethical methods that have worked for others, even if they are off the beaten path. Why not move heaven and earth in certain circumstances? On the other hand, we need not feel obliged to try out extraordinary treatments. We should feel free to say "no" if the costs are too high for us, emotionally speaking and otherwise. At certain times, we might want to take a break from trying out yet another approach. Or perhaps we are ready to turn the page.

The difficulty often lies with having to live with our decisions in the long term. It is tempting to mull things over obsessively and ask ourselves whether if we'd only tried out x, y, and z, we might perhaps have had one or more children. It's easy to torture ourselves with these questions. Therefore, it is important to make these decisions in front of God. Being finite beings, we cannot predict or guess all the consequences of our choices. It is good therefore to ask God for guidance and entrust our choices to Him. Perhaps we won't have a baby and perhaps other decisions would have been better. God does not necessarily protect us from all error. But by asking Him to show us the way, we allow Him to be in charge of our life with all its difficulties and unforeseen outcomes, and it is easier to gain interior peace.[2]

However, we ought to research our options and choose the most promising ones with prudence. God does not guarantee us children—nor good health, a satisfying job, a spouse, and so forth. That would be reducing Him to playing the role of a gift-giver in the sky bestowing a health and wealth gospel that promises an earthly paradise. If we hope for that, we will surely be disappointed. On the other hand, He will not fail us; He assures us that everything will "[work] for good with those who love him" (Rom 8:28). The Cross is part of our human condition as is the fallibility of our decisions.

Assuming the Best when Others Hurt Us

When other people hurt us by their ill-chosen comments, it is good to keep in mind that they may well not know how painful infertility is. Perhaps they feel insecure, don't know how to react, and say the first thing that comes to mind, not realizing the implications of their comments. They carry their own wounds, and our trial may stir up painful memories such as an abortion, the loss of a child, or their own infertility. Perhaps their pain was not sufficiently acknowledged and therefore, in talking to us, their own suffering, bitterness, and resentment resurfaces. Just as our situation is a challenge to them to be compassionate, so their

---

[2] I recommend the powerful "surrender novena," during which we surrender everything to Jesus who can only fully help us if we entrust every worry to Him. It was put together by St. Padre Pio's confessor, a certain Padre Dolindo, of whom Padre Pio said that he had heaven in his heart. "The Surrender Novena by Fr. Dolindo Ruotolo (1882–1970)," Novena Prayer, May 26, 2020, https://novenaprayer.com/2020/05/26/the-surrender-novena-by-father-dolindo-ruotolo-1882-1970/.

lack of understanding and unfortunate words are a call for us to be generous in granting forgiveness and to be understanding. Remembering how we have lacked tact toward other people in the past and have probably added to their burdens can help us to be more forgiving.

Trying to Fill the Emptiness

To escape from the frustrating and seemingly futile waiting time for a child, I might attempt to fill the void with other things. Though work, travel, or other occupations are a good idea and certainly better than remaining depressed at home all day long, I shouldn't expect them to cure me if I haven't gone through the process of mourning. Then these escapes will only give a brief respite, preventing me from going through the pain and making it impossible for God to be present in my grief. As the divine doctor, He needs to touch my wounds to heal them. But if I don't give Him access by remaining still and creating some inner space, He won't be able to do so. And then I won't find inner peace; instead, exhaustion and depression will be the likely consequences. Therefore, times of quiet prayer are necessary in the midst of our activities.

Divine Mindreading

Part of the difficulty of suffering is that it seems so pointless, so devoid of meaning. It is tempting to desire meaning at all costs rather than letting it disclose itself by growing closer to Christ. In a way, it is an attempt to read God's mind or, like Job's "friends" in the Old Testament, to impose intelligibility on a situation that is quite inexplicable. Thus, couples are sometimes tempted to think that perhaps they would not have been good parents or that God is punishing them for something.

This can be particularly appealing, for example, for women who have become infertile after an abortion, or who have taken the Pill for many years (a practice which might have caused a hormonal imbalance), or for women who simply put their career first and waited too long to have children. Those suffering from the aftereffects of an abortion often need to go through a long, inner healing process. The group Rachel's Vineyard, for example, offers retreats that help people come to terms with this wound.[3] Part of the healing process is to ask God for forgiveness, to come to realize which factors in myself and my surroundings led to this decision, to ask my child for forgiveness, and to give them a name and entrust them to God. Eventually I will be able to accept God's forgiveness and also forgive myself. It is a long and difficult process. But there too, peace can be found, even though the pain may be long-lasting.

God is quick to forgive; He waits for our return and comes running toward us when we are still far away, as the parable of the Prodigal Son shows. He pardons us much sooner than we are able to forgive ourselves. He is the only one who can give us true peace after such tragic choices whose consequences will accompany us for the rest of our lives. He alone knows us to the core of our being and is capable of satisfying our infinite longing for love.

But if we try to do this kind of divine mind-reading, chances are high we won't get it right. Bearing the apparent meaninglessness of suffering, that is, undergoing a dark night, is part of the mystery of the Cross. Trying to escape it at all costs is spiritually

---

[3] See their website, Rachel's Vineyard, accessed November 10, 2020, http://www.rachelsvineyard.org/.

sterile. Sometimes God gives us an insight into why He allows certain kinds of suffering. But let us not artificially try to impose reasons that are ultimately hurtful to us and may twist our perception of God's loving goodness.

Though everything works toward the good of those who love God, as St. Paul already said, and though this suffering will be part of our salvation and perhaps essential to it, there is a way of focusing on suffering and its place in God's plan which is unhealthy and contradicts God's love. Because of original sin, we tend to distrust God and see in Him a tyrant rather than a loving father. The way to avoid this is to contemplate Him in adoration or mental prayer. Suffering can draw us into a dark vortex and make us doubt God's love rather than help us unite ourselves with Him. Trying to read God's mind means evading the real issue (which is to unite ourselves to Him) and ascribing to Him motives that are all too human. Rather than attempting to figure out why this is happening to me and what God's plans are through all of this, I will find it much more fruitful to make an act of trust. For if I stick to Him and hold out through this dark night, I will come to see that He was with me all along, and that nothing can separate me from His infinite love.

ENVY OR SIMPLY PAIN?

In the meantime, I can all too easily have very human reactions. I am tempted to compare my situation to that of others who have no trouble conceiving and to feel envious and misunderstood because they don't seem to have a clue about what I am going through. It is particularly hard when others are announcing a new pregnancy. Though I do not wish to spoil someone else's joy over their baby, it can be a very painful moment. Yet there is a time for everything, and this is not one to bring up my own pain. These moments may call for heroism—like keeping a smile on my face—though afterwards I can allow myself to mourn and express my sorrow to my spouse.

However, perhaps I am wrongly taking my pain for envy. My suffering will surge at certain times, especially when seeing the children of others, but this is not yet envy, though it might lead to it. It is simply triggered by these occasions.[4] But if it is envy, then focusing on God's mercy toward me is key, while telling myself that I should not feel envy is futile. On the contrary, envy will simply "go underground" while being very much alive, disguising itself perhaps in an accentuated critical spirit, resentment, or anger that will explode at other moments. Confessing it to a priest and asking God to free me from this scourge will cut at its roots, even if I might struggle with it for a long time. And at the risk of repeating myself, mourning my infertility keeps this wound from festering and leading to bitterness.

Given every person's unique individuality, everyone has a call and path that are specifically his or her own. Others have their own crosses and we don't know how they feel or how they struggle with them. Another who seems to be doing very well might in reality be in the depths of despair and will need our compassion, while our own envy only increases his loneliness. As René Girard showed so well, envy (or mimetic desire, as he calls it) suggests that the other possesses absolute happiness and complete autonomy. This makes us blind to the fact that everyone feels incomplete, that there is no absolute happiness in this world, and that the only one capable of fulfilling our infinite desire, as St. Augustine expressed

---

[4] By the way, not mourning my childlessness will most likely increase the danger of envy. Instead of facing my pain, I will, in all likelihood, focus on the other whose happiness I'd like to enjoy.

so well, is God. Neither the other nor what he possesses can satisfy us ultimately. Yes, of course, having children seems like absolute bliss! But even children will not satisfy us completely.

In the meantime, if I am incapable of feeling happy for others when they announce their pregnancies, I can throw myself into the arms of God and come running with my pain to Him. For He knows how intense it is, how it breaks me, and how difficult it is not to have what I desire most. Focusing on another person's life is going to distort my perspective and cloud God's call for me in this particular situation. Though God will probably not explain in a theoretical way why He is allowing this particular suffering, His answer, as John Paul II explains in *Salvifici Doloris*, will be a call and a vocation; it will become my unique path to holiness.[5]

Judging Those Who Fail to Be Supportive

When one has been hurt by the ill-placed comments of others, it can be tempting to judge them. But I cannot know why the other is unable to tell me something consoling and instead is adding insult to injury. I can easily judge them as being insensitive and unchari-table. But I cannot fully know why the other cannot say the right thing. Perhaps they are simply tactless, lack psychological finesse, or have a hard time empathizing. Perhaps they feel overwhelmed, paralyzed, and helpless. This can strike them mute and dumb, or make them say the first thing that comes to mind—which turns out to be hurtful. There might be many reasons in their character and life of which I am perhaps unaware and which might make them blameless in the eyes of God.

---

[5] Pope John Paul II, Apostolic Letter on the Christian Meaning of Human Suffering *Salvifici Doloris* (February 11, 1984), § 26 (hereafter cited in text as SD).

Furthermore, I need to choose wisely with whom to share my experience. If some members of the family lack tact or I don't get along with them very well, then there is no reason why I should open up to them and invite a bad reaction. Charity does not require it, and might well be served best by not putting our relationship under any further strain. No one has a right to be "let" into the inner forum of my pain, nor should I feel pressured by the expectations of others. They might feel disappointment or judge me as being aloof or closed up, but so be it.

Instead, I should choose a good friend, a wise priest, or a good counselor who knows how to listen well and give sound advice. For suffering has a way of bubbling up, wanting to surface at any time, whether the people around me are particularly compassionate or not. But if I can pour out my heart to one or a few empathetic people gifted with wisdom, then I will be less tempted to put myself at risk by sharing my pain with the whole world.

Though I should not judge those who have hurt me by their words and acts, it is a fact that I have been hurt. I should not deny this but take the time I might need to forgive them. For forgiveness cannot be forced; neither by the other nor by me. It is a grace I need to ask from God. To create a certain distance from the other might be a good idea, if feasible; for this gives me the time and distance to forgive more easily rather than receive new wounds added to the old ones.

THE STRAIN ON THE COUPLE

To suffer from infertility can be a huge burden for the couple that can lead to a marital crisis. Men and women have very different ways of approaching problems and addressing suffering. Women tend to need to talk more about their pain, explain their frustrations and cry over the absence of children. Men, in contrast, frequently want to find a solution without saying much. A husband does not want to see his wife suffer, and he becomes frustrated when he cannot resolve the issue. His wife's approach seems futile to him, and it might be difficult for him to understand why she wants to speak about it so often.

The danger is real for each to close their heart to the other, the wife thinking her husband's silence reveals an indifference to her suffering and a hardness of heart. The husband, in contrast, might come to the conclusion that his wife is overly sensitive; not wanting to encourage this by further dwelling on their infertility, he fails to talk to her. Everything is now in place for a major crisis. Each one suffers on his own, and to the pain of infertility is now added the suffering of a lack of communion between the spouses.

It is therefore essential that the spouses realize that the other experiences and approaches this pain differently. It is important for both to acknowledge this, but also to reach out to each other. The husband should create the space for his wife to express her anguish while she should not oblige him to speak about his, even though she can encourage him. If he is silent, then this doesn't mean that he doesn't care. It's more likely he feels helpless. The most productive approach could be for her to let him know what she needs and how much it helps her when she can share with him how she experiences the situation. At the same time, one spouse is often in greater pain than the other. There too, reaching out to the other is essential. Feeling less pain in this circumstance need not be the sign of hardheartedness, but simply having a less strong desire for children or a happier predisposition.

The wife ought also to tell her husband that his presence at various gynecological appointments would be of great support to her. It is difficult for her to find herself in a waiting room filled with pregnant women. It is tough to get bad news from the doctor on one's own, or perhaps to be pressured to try IVF. Hence, she experiences it as very supportive when her husband researches medical options with his wife rather than letting her do everything on her own. Together they should look for good doctors whom they can trust. And when pain paralyzes the woman and makes her incapable of taking action, then the husband can take things in hand.

Some even go so far as to divorce and remarry in order to fulfill their dream of a child. This is a terrible rejection of my spouse to whom I promised faithfulness under all circumstances. It means the instrumentalization of my new partner, who becomes the "means" for me to have children. Love has been betrayed, and the children coming out of this new relationship are born into a utilitarian environment.

However, the experience of infertility can also bind the spouses more strongly together when they are capable of expressing to each other their sufferings and their needs, to accept the other in their physiological or emotional fragility. What an extraordinary thing it is to tell each other that I choose the other every day anew as my spouse, even if the original project of having (many) children will not be realized.[6]

---

[6] Jameson Taylor, *This Rock* (El Cajon, CA: Catholic Answers, 2006), 16–24, quoted in "Babies Deserve Better," Catholic Culture, Trinity Communications, accessed October 12, 2020, https://www.catholicculture.org/culture /library/view.cfm?recnum=6984. When we get married, we choose each other with our fertility (except in the case of known sterility). We promise to accept the children God will send us and as practicing Catholics refuse to use contraception. In his theology of the body, St. John Paul II speaks about the language of the body capable of expressing love. A caress already shows love, while sexual union expresses a complete gift of self. So, if I give myself to another without being married, my body has lied. It tells him that I belong to him while in reality we have not committed ourselves to one another through

marriage. Similarly, contraception introduces a lie within the union, for we give ourselves to the other only partially, that is, by excluding our fertility, while our bodies say otherwise. The sexual act thus becomes a lie and hurts love in its very heart; Pope John Paul II, *Man and Woman He Created Them: A Theology of the Body*, trans. Michael Waldstein (Boston, MA: Pauline Books and Media, 2006) 123:6–7 (pp. 632–633). It is therefore not surprising that the disobedience of Catholics to *Humanae Vitae*—though its teaching was rendered so clearly later on by Pope John Paul II—leads to the destruction of the family. Divorce and abortion are its consequences.

Chapter 3

WHAT NOT TO SAY: SOME ADVICE
TO FAMILY AND FRIENDS

Families and friends often feel helpless as they see their loved ones going through this trial. They witness their pain, or worse, sense their eventual withdrawal. Family members and friends would love to know how to help, relieve them of this burden, or at least alleviate it, but don't seem to know the secret. Relationships become strained or even break, and more sadness is added to an already tragic situation.

I will give you a few principles for navigating this situation, mainly by showing what *not* to do, but thereby also uncovering the underlying attitude that will guide you like a compass through these difficulties. With the best of intentions, one can end up hurting the infertile couple through one's advice or comments, inadvertently making their situation worse. Most of these hurtful incidents can be easily avoided.

Don't Give Any Unasked-For Advice

First of all, we can more easily hurt people suffering from infertility by saying something rather than nothing. We should not feel that we have to give advice. If the right thing does not come to mind, then it is better to listen with compassion, saying simple things such as, "I am so sorry you are undergoing such pain." If this comes from the heart, then it will be very soothing. Often, we would like to give some kind of pertinent counsel that will liberate people from their suffering. But in all likelihood, nothing we are going to say is going to resolve their problem. Instead, showing empathy speaks to the heart rather than to the mind, and is therefore most likely to be truly consoling. We may not feel like we have done anything helpful since we haven't been able to remove their pain, but it will give the kind of encouragement that makes the journey bearable. Simon of Cyrene could not liberate Christ from the Cross, but he helped Him carry it.

Don't Bring Up the Topic

In ninety-nine cases out of one hundred, I would recommend not broaching the subject. The person concerned may not want to talk about it at the moment or perhaps simply not with you, and this should be respected. The couple's infertility is a very sore topic, and bringing it up when they are either in great pain or—for the moment—happily not thinking about it may not be helpful.

If they mention it, then this is different, and listening to them with attention and compassion will bring some relief and is a true work of mercy. However, if you are close to the couple or one of the spouses, you may indicate that you're happy to talk about it, if they so wish, but that this is completely up to them and that you do not want to exert any pressure whatsoever.

Some may ask, though, whether there isn't an obligation to make sure the couple is not contracepting or using natural family planning when they ought not to. I have found it ironic that even my husband and I have been approached in that way despite our pro-life commitment and my husband's longtime work for a pro-life organization. Additionally, an infertile friend of mine who worked in the pro-life movement had similarly been asked why she was doing this work instead of having children and staying at home. This is adding insult to injury. It is important to realize that if you are not close to the couple or if you are not in a position of spiritual authority (such as a priest), then it is not your task to raise that issue, except if it comes up naturally. While the infertile couple would be tempted to react in an uncharitable way to such nosey questions, my husband and I decided to answer along the lines of: "We are very sad not to have children. Could you please pray for us?"

CURIOSITY

Furthermore, I'd like to emphasize the importance of avoiding curiosity. I have found that some people would love to know the reason for one's infertility. Being asked about the reason for one's childlessness and sensing that curiosity is a motivating factor is painful. Instead of receiving sympathy, one becomes the victim of voyeurism. Being a topic for gossip, or simply an idle news item, is very jarring. I found it hurtful to be asked what my medical issues were, assuming that the problem must have been me rather than my husband.

Stories along the lines of, "Once I (or someone else) had given up the hope of having children, I became pregnant" are less than helpful. This may be true, or the reason for the pregnancy may have been different and one just doesn't know it: the point is that this kind of story seems to insinuate that the woman is obviously not detached or not abandoned to God's will, for otherwise she, too, would have conceived. Stress—and there is a lot of stress that builds up with infertility—may be an important factor. But people don't become less stressed by being told not to be stressed. Frequently, all that is achieved is making them stressed about being stressed.

WALKING ON EGGSHELLS

It may seem like you have to walk on eggshells around infertile couples. It can seem almost impossible to talk to them without hurting them. No! Please do not get this impression, though it is good to try to be sensitive as to how you come across.

It is true that with certain couples, the mere allusion to a birth or baptism will be painful. Their suffering is obviously great, but you cannot take responsibility for their pain either, not even for that which has been caused inadvertently. Everyone has their own wounds, and there is always the risk of stirring them up without being aware of doing so.

Whatever may be the case, if you are motivated by charity, then even clumsy mistakes will probably not hurt the couple in the same way as those who manifest hardness of heart or lack compassion. This kind of situation is a school of love for both sides. By recognizing our own wounds, we are more willing to forgive another. And if others react badly, it helps to realize that their anger has its source in pain.

Hence, tactlessness or a wrong comment are perhaps the expression of another person's own wounds and ill-lived sufferings. Infertile couples as well as the people surrounding them need to learn how to forgive each other, even if in this situation the first are more often the ones sinned against than the latter. For they are in a position of great vulnerability, their pain being very raw.

Perhaps more common to our experience is to have unmarried friends who suffer tremendously from being single. We will still talk about our husbands or wives or current joys and pains arising from our family life around them. At the same time, we probably will be sensitive enough not to gush too much about our spouses, how wonderful it is to be married, and so on, if we know that this causes greater pain.

INVITATIONS TO BAPTISMS AND BABY SHOWERS

What should people do about invitations to baby showers and baptisms vis-à-vis infertile couples? This question leaves many who would like to avoid hurting those suffering from infertility as much as possible feeling puzzled. My experience has been that it is good to invite them to these events, otherwise they might feel excluded. At the same time, the infertile couple should feel free to turn down the invitation if it is too difficult for them. And people should not be offended if infertile couples don't accept their invitation, even if they are closely related (for example siblings).[1] The pain may simply be too strong, especially after many years of infertility.

Again, one should avoid suggesting to the couple that they should really be over their pain by this point and that they should pull themselves together, at the very least out of love for their family or friends. We simply cannot judge what they are going

---

[1] Carmen Santamaría and Angelique Rúhi-Lopez also give this advice in their comprehensive book *The Infertility Companion for Catholics* (Miami, FL: Ave Maria Press, 2012), p. 180.

through. Rather than sending them on a guilt trip, it is much more helpful to tell them how much their presence would give one joy, but that they should feel free to come or not. To put pressure on them not only shows a lack of charity, but the risk is great that the celebration might be affected by their pain and resentment at having been forced to come.

As I already mentioned, those who are suffering from infertility should feel free to turn these invitations down. If the invitations are not from close friends or family members, then they can do so without further explanation. If it requires some justification, then they can simply state that they are very sorry not to be able to come, but that it is too painful at the moment and that this is no reflection on their joy for the friend or family member.

At the same time, I might want to ask myself each time whether I don't have it in myself to go to this baptism or baby shower, even if it is very painful. Perhaps this is a challenge I am now capable of facing. If people see me cry, well then, so be it. This could be a wake-up call for them as to how great a suffering this is. Or perhaps, by the grace of God, attending the baptism or baby shower may not be as difficult as envisaged.

I remember going to the baptism of a niece after seven years of infertility. The Benedictine priest, who did not seem to have much pastoral experience with this suffering, spent the whole sermon speaking about how a woman feels the love of God most strongly when she is having a child. This left the childless women present (and I was not the only one) out in the rain. Normally, I would have been cut in two from these words. However, for some reason, I was able to shake it off and simply say to myself that this priest was not only very insensitive but also downright wrong. For where does that leave the many childless saints, nuns, or simply unmarried women who never had biological children? Does it make sense that God would not let them experience His love for them as strongly as those women giving birth?

Let me conclude this point by emphasizing that there is no right or wrong answer to these kinds of invitations. It depends simply on each individual case and what God is calling me to do at the moment; perhaps God is asking me to be gentle on myself and not put myself in a painful situation, or He may be challenging me to do so. This is between me and God, and it is not about what others think.

This poem used by Mother Teresa can be of real help in these circumstances:[2]

People are often unreasonable, illogical, and self-centered;
Forgive them anyway.
If you are kind, people may accuse you of selfish, ulterior motives;
Be kind anyway.
If you are successful, you will win some
false friends and some true enemies;
Succeed anyway.
If you are honest and frank, people may cheat you;
Be honest and frank anyway.
What you spend years building,
someone could destroy overnight;
Build anyway.
If you find serenity and happiness, they may be jealous;
Be happy anyway.
The good you do today, people will often forget tomorrow;
Do good anyway.
Give the world the best you have, and it may never be enough;

---

[2] The original version of this poem, "Anyway," comes from Dr. Kent M. Keith.

Give the world the best you've got anyway.
You see, in the final analysis, it is between you and your God;
It was never between you and them anyway.

Yes, all of this only concerns God and me: it's my story, not that of others; it's my cross and only God can judge if I carry it well according to His design. If I give a bad impression, or if I seem to be lacking in courage or faith in the eyes of others, it doesn't matter. God knows my heart and my difficulties; He knows my suffering. The important point is to become His child without worrying how others judge me, to know myself loved by God and to abandon myself to His will.

How to Announce a Pregnancy

Another sensitive topic is how to announce my pregnancy to my infertile friends. I don't want this happy news to make them suffer, yet I know that pain will be the inevitable result.

I had better not wait until the last minute, hoping that they will learn through a third party or see it with their own eyes. Personally, I prefer emails to the phone or face to face. Don't be afraid that an email might not be personal enough. It is! It is much easier to go through this new mourning process and be able to answer with real joy to the happy news afterwards, rather than having to pull oneself together to hide the pain this is triggering. Consider also (if you happen to know) where the infertile couple is at that moment. I'd avoid breaking the news when the woman suffering from infertility is at her mother-in-law's, where she might well not feel free to show her pain and has to put on a brave face.

A friend of mine who had been suffering from infertility for many years announced her pregnancy in an email, mentioning that this happy news might well be painful for those without children to hear. This gesture touched me and showed that she hadn't forgotten what it was like to get this kind of announcement.

BLAMING THE VICTIM

It is tempting to become like Job's friends in the Old Testament. When experiencing great suffering, we are prone to make the other responsible for their pain. For a while, we are willing to commiserate, to be there for the suffering person. Then it becomes tedious to be standing under the Cross for so long without any sign of improvement. We start looking for reasons for this long-lasting trial, somehow trying to make them responsible for it or for their failure to get over it. This appears in such subtle forms that we can find it hard to put our finger on it.

The philosopher Simone Weil explains that this is so because naturally speaking we cannot bear suffering; we try to avoid it at all costs, and it is easier to blame someone for it rather than bearing it together with the other person. "Thought flees affliction as promptly," Weil writes, "and as irresistibly as an animal flees death." And she adds: "Man has carnal nature in common with animals. Hens throw themselves on a[n already] wounded hen, pecking on her with their beaks."[3]

Thus, we will be tempted to think that it is in some way the infertile woman's fault, that she is too stressed or not sufficiently abandoned to God's will; or perhaps that she obviously needed this cross, that she deserved it somehow if God is sending it to her. The temptation to do so is particularly strong if there has been

---

[3] Simone Weil, *Œuvres complètes*, bk. 4, vol. 1: *Écrits de Marseille (1940–1942)*, ed. Monique Broc-Lapeyre et al. (Paris: Gallimard, 2008), pp. 346–374, 348, 350. Translations of Simone Weil into English are my own.

some fault such as a previous abortion or the use of contraception. But remember: the sufferings of the person concerned are not any less if there is any previous culpability. On the contrary, feelings of guilt and worthlessness are added to the suffering of infertility and make the experience all the more painful. Compassion is needed, not another guilt trip!

If the couple has decided against IVF for ethical reasons, family and friends should respect their decision at the very least, even if they don't understand it. But their approval will be a real encouragement for the couple on their journey, since they will probably experience pressure and blame from others not understanding their choice. Hopefully the explanation in chapters four and five will make clearer why this decision is not only ethically right, but a choice that conforms to the dignity of the human persons involved who need to be approached with love at all times.

"It's Not the End of the World"

One may also get impatient with the couple for not getting "over it" after years of waiting. But it is not for anyone to determine how long another person's time of mourning should take. Everyone is different. To insinuate that the couple should really have dealt with this by now, that other sufferings are a lot worse, that so-and-so who is so sick never complains, is less than helpful: it tells the couple that their suffering has no right to exist, that they should repress it.

Similarly, women who have had miscarriages or abortions suffer from the fact that they are not given any or enough time to mourn. It takes a long time to find healing. Even if you have the impression that the other person is wallowing in self-pity, it does not help her deal with her pain if you tell her she should stop being upset.

In contrast, to be willing to listen and empathize with her is a tremendous consolation to the suffering. However, if I feel tired or impatient, it is better to withdraw, explaining perhaps that I'm not well and unfortunately not able to help the other just now. Everyone has their limits. We ought to recognize and admit them. No one is superman or superwoman; no one can be available at all times. We need some time to recharge our batteries. To ignore this is a recipe for disaster: impatience will ensue and more hurt will be the consequence.

For impatience is a form of anger. By implying that I have had enough "of your complaining, of your running around in circles," I am manifesting anger toward the other, which is very destructive. Even when silent, impatience makes itself felt and reveals itself through small gestures and inflections. It provokes new wounds in someone who is already hurting much.

To be able to bear with another in their pain, I need the supernatural virtue of *caritas*, that is, divine love of neighbor. Natural goodness and altruism have their limits. Only *caritas* is infinite, for it finds its source in God. It allows me to love another in their suffering despite their faults, weaknesses, and apparent ugliness. Every person is a universe of their own with an abyss of pain. They are a child of God, a sister, a brother. They partake of the Passion of Christ, becoming similar to Him. By helping them, we succor Him.

One day, St. Faustina helped a beggar who came to her convent. He then showed Himself to be Christ.[4] Something

---

[4] St. Maria Faustina Kowalska, *Diary: Divine Mercy in My Soul* (Stockbridge, MA: Marians of the Immaculate Conception, 2001), no. 1312.

similar happened to a priest who came to help the dying with the Missionaries of Charity. He shared with Mother Teresa that he had really seen Christ, that a sick person had been transformed into Him in front of his eyes. "Ah, you too have seen Him," she replied.

Adoption Isn't Always the Solution

Adoption sounds like a great option for couples suffering from infertility, and it certainly is. However, it's not for everyone. It is a vocation in and of itself, and not every infertile couple has this call. Many couples suffering from infertility would like to adopt but cannot because they don't meet the criteria or because there are simply not enough children available. Friends of mine went through the process five times, yet every time the adoption fell through. Those who have experience with the process know what a heartache this is. My friends soon understood that God was simply not calling them to be parents. It was difficult for them to accept; yet they have now found inner peace and are involved in various ministries.

There is a right and a wrong way of suggesting adoption to a couple struggling with infertility. It would be wrong to assume that the issue will be resolved through adoption or that the couple's pain will thereby evaporate. Women have told me how hurtful this suggestion was. There is a great blessing in being procreators, in bearing one's own children, and it is a suffering not to have that option. Couples do not love their adopted children less than those born to them. And yet they often still suffer from not bearing children themselves.

COMPASSION, NOT ACCUSATION

The most healing thing that can be done for those who suffer is to suffer with them. This is the true meaning of being compassionate, which comes from the Latin word *compati*: *pati*, meaning to bear, to suffer, and *com*, to do so with the other.[5] We should be with suffering persons where they are. It is presumptuous to start by trying to pull them up to where we think they should be. Finding fault with them for suffering, for not doing things we think they should, or accusing them of envy are all ways of blaming the victim and making matters worse for them. This may again be a way of avoiding suffering oneself, of not wanting to spend this time with the other in their pain.

I once read that St. Mother Teresa was asked about her secret to helping the suffering. Even well-to-do families asked her to open a hospice in the United States for those suffering from AIDS, knowing that she could truly assist them as they lay dying. Her secret was to stand under the Cross with them. This means sharing their suffering, or telling them that you love them enough to remain with them even in this difficult time of perhaps unbearable pain and anguish as Our Lady and St. John the Evangelist did under Christ's Cross.

Sometimes this is the only thing that is left when all other avenues have been tried. But this is also the testing ground for love, for transcendence of self. It is much easier to try to "fix the problem" and thereby remain an outsider to the other person's suffering. But now is the moment when our mettle is being tested. This is only possible if we draw our strength from Christ; St. Mother Teresa therefore taught her Missionaries of Charity

---

[5] Originally the word comes from the Greek *pascho*, which takes on new significance through Christ's Passion.

to spend long hours in adoration to be able to do their work. As Simone Weil wrote, "The capacity to pay attention to someone afflicted is something very rare, very difficult; it is almost a miracle; it is a miracle. Almost all those who believe they have this skill don't have it. Warmth, a heartfelt impulse, pity are not enough."[6] Instead of having less time for the patients, the missionaries had more once they started spending an extra hour in adoration. For they were even more present, calmer, and more loving. Only God can give us the strength to embrace our cross and to help others carry theirs.[7]

Therefore, if we wish to give counsel in any situation, we must always ask ourselves the following questions: is our motive really a desire to help others? Or do we simply want our peace and quiet from their moans and groans? Furthermore, we have to make sure that we are not merely gratifying our own pride from which we derive the false sense of being on a mission to "save" another.

If our motivation is unambiguously to console the other person, we have to make sure that we meet the other where they are emotionally and spiritually, whether they are at this point

---

[6] "Réflexions sur le bon usage des études scolaires en vue de l'amour de Dieu," in Weil, *Œuvres complètes*, bk. 4, vol. 1: *Écrits de Marseille*, pp. 255–262, p. 262.

[7] At the core of many wrong responses to other people's pain is the desire to run away, not to stand under that cross with them. Telling stories about sufferings that are worse than theirs sends them the message that their pain is not worth acknowledging compared to that of others, and that they do not have the right to mourn. A friend of mine who lost her child just two weeks before giving birth was told about other people who had lost children too; but since those children had already been born, their suffering was presented as being much worse than hers. Instead of being consoled, she was, in a way, being reprimanded for being so upset. However, hearing the witnesses of other people who lived through great crises can be very helpful, if those suffering are at a point where they are ready to hear them and if these stories are told with an inspirational purpose in mind rather than for the above-mentioned reason.

wrongly or rightly; otherwise, nothing we say will have an impact and we will simply be satisfying a personal urge by trying to give counsel. In her talk, "Pastoring with Strength and Compassion," Dr. Maria Fedoryka makes the following excellent point:

> Suffering with the one who suffers represents a particular summit of love. The warmth of love, its tenderness, its gentle regard, are revealed with particular clarity in the willingness to suffer with another. Because in order to suffer with another, I have to enter into the other with utmost reverence, being attentive to *his* heart, being attuned to what *he* is feeling, truly *understanding his* experience as *other*, and different from myself. As long as we "objectivize" the other, as long as we impose on him our categories, our way of seeing and feeling, we will never be able to offer genuine compassion. Once again: we must offer an unconditional affirmation of the one who suffers.[8]

One thing is certain, and everyone has experienced this at some point or other: most of us know if another is really trying to help and is responding lovingly or not, even if we may not be able to put into words at that moment what the other is doing right or wrong.

When someone opens up to me, then I am walking on "holy ground." Prudence, humility, wisdom, and love are required. And if nothing comes to mind, words of compassion, of shared sorrow over the other person's pain, will work wonders.

---

[8] Dr. Maria Fedoryka, "Pastoring with Strength and Compassion" (lecture, Ave Maria University Pastors' Workshop "Priest, Prophet, and King: Pastoring in Today's Church," Naples, FL, February 2006).

So the answer of how to help those suffering from infertility couldn't be simpler or more obvious: love. But between knowing this and putting it into practice lies a chasm. For it is primarily not a question of understanding, but of transformation of heart. And that takes time and is a painful process. The kinks in our heart manifest themselves in these circumstances and should become turning points once we realize that we are not quite as loving as we imagined. For a stone is easier to melt than a hardened heart.

Chapter 4

GOD'S LOVING PLAN FOR US: THE CHURCH'S ANTHROPOLOGICAL AND ETHICAL APPROACH

From the beginning, God had a wonderful plan for us. Adam cried out in joy upon seeing Eve, calling her flesh of his flesh. God blessed their union and told them to become one and to be fertile. So not only were Adam and Eve given to each other, but God entrusted them with the awe-inspiring mission of begetting children—a fruitfulness flowing directly from their communion of love. Though original sin then created a tectonic rift between human beings and God, between each other, and between them and nature, the call to marriage and parenting has not changed— it has only become difficult and is easily wounded by sin (see CCC 1607–1608).

Love is essentially fruitful—it spreads goodness.[1] Even more,

---

[1] Pope John Paul II, *Man and Woman He Created Them*, 16:1 (p. 190): "Only

spousal love can lead to the coming-into-being of another human person with the help of God, who creates each soul individually. The spouses become co-creators participating in this great mystery of life. Since "children are the supreme gift of marriage and contribute greatly to the good of the parents themselves," as *Gaudium et Spes* states, the spouses' frustration and pain are therefore potentially immense when no children or less than they would have hoped for are born.[2] The couple suffering from infertility can feel stunted in their vocation, deprived of what feels like the blooming and external expression of their love for each other. They may believe that their life's plan has been wrecked.

The Help of Science and God's Lifegiving Law

But God has inscribed into nature the means of healing illnesses. Science discovers these and can bring wholeness to people's broken bodies. It is a great comfort to couples suffering from infertility to be given options to overcome their condition.

Though science is a wonderful tool, it is not without its problems. Science needs ethics as desperately as explorers need their compass. Frankenstein's creation of the monster in Mary Shelley's novel is a prophetic warning for our times. Most agree that science is in need of some control and guidelines. Therefore, ethical considerations (whether a procedure goes against the life

---

Love creates the good." And what John Paul II calls "the hermeneutics of the gift" in the same place is a way of looking at creation as God's gift to human beings who are called in their turn to give themselves.

2 Pope Paul VI, Pastoral Constitution on the Church in the Modern World *Gaudium et Spes* (December 7, 1965), § 50 (hereafter cited as GS), quoted in CCC 1652.

and dignity of the persons involved or not) should be applied to all medical approaches and scientific experiments, for fear they might be wanting.

God did not leave us helpless in the face of illness after the Fall; nor did He abandon us to face evil defenselessly before His salvific redemption. The natural moral law that He inscribed into our hearts, as St. Paul says, gives us the guidance necessary to navigate the stormy seas of temptation and confusion. It helps us enact the language of love that we so easily forget.

However, because of our woundedness, the waters get muddied and we lose our clear vision of this law, especially when our self-interest is involved or when the issues at stake are complicated. Furthermore, we tend to experience God's moral commands not only as a burden, but as something that stunts us, making human happiness impossible. In reality, His commands are life-giving and ultimately fulfilling, even if they require self-sacrifice. They protect us from the worst in us when we are tempted to break our promises because of suffering, pride, or concupiscence, all in the desperate attempt to find (false) fulfillment and solace from our inner feeling of want. As *Donum Vitae* rightly states: "For it is out of goodness—in order to indicate the path of life—that God gives human beings his commandments and the grace to observe them."[3] So not only does He give us laws to help us lead a good life, but He also gives us the grace to do so. Receiving the sacraments and prayer are ways to obtain the help we need.

---

[3] Congregation for the Doctrine of the Faith, Instruction on Respect for Human Life in Its Origin and on the Dignity of Procreation *Donum Vitae* (February 22, 1987), introduction, § 1 (hereafter cited in text as DV).

MADE FOR LOVE

As St. John Paul II so beautifully brought to light in his theology of the body, men and women have a nuptial meaning inscribed into their very bodies, indicating their complementarity, as they are both made in the image of God.[4] They are meant for gift of self within lifelong marriage. Only this lifelong commitment allows for self-donation, since a gift that would be limited merely to a certain period from the outset or to certain conditions ("as long as I'm in love, things aren't difficult," etc.) would not be unconditional, and therefore not really love at all.[5] Deep down we all crave this kind of love—to be accepted, warts and all—even if disappointments may have led us to become cynical.

However, not only those who get married, but all human beings have the vocation to gift of self.[6] Priests, religious, and consecrated make this gift of themselves to God; their celibacy is an expression of this total self-gift to Him. But also, those who remain unmarried without a vocation to the consecrated life are called to self-donation that can express itself in many forms.

Human beings want nothing more than to be loved completely

---

[4] Pope John Paul II, *Man and Woman He Created Them*, 15:1 (pp. 185–186): "This freedom [to give themselves] lies exactly at the basis of the spousal meaning of the body. The human body, with its sex—its masculinity and femininity—seen in the very mystery of creation, is not only a source of fruitfulness and of procreation, as in the whole natural order, but contains 'from the beginning' the 'spousal' attribute, that is, *the power to express love: precisely that love in which the human person becomes a gift* and—through this gift—fulfills the very meaning of his being and existence."

[5] "Love seeks to be definitive; it cannot be an arrangement 'until further notice.' The 'intimate union of marriage, as a mutual giving of two persons, and the good of the children, demand total fidelity from the spouses and require an unbreakable union between them.'" CCC 1646, referencing GS 48.

[6] "For man is created in the image and likeness of God who is himself love." CCC 1604.

and unconditionally throughout their life. Original sin has made that difficult. We are often disappointed in our hope to be loved while falling short of it ourselves. Love since the Fall requires death to self. The Cross is therefore at the heart of love this side of eternity—and that is true for Christians and non-Christians alike. Otherwise, both eros and agape turn stale through one's egoism, leading to anger, possessiveness, hatred, and separation (see CCC 1606, 1615).

Hence, the call to marriage is challenging. But through Christ's institution of the sacrament of marriage, as John Paul II so beautifully stated, the spouses can return to God's original plan, that is, the way marriage and sexuality were intended from the beginning. And what better setting is there than marriage for the begetting of children who need to be surrounded by love from the first instant of their existence? Their parents' love is their cradle. Their vulnerability heightens their need for unconditional love. And which parents, whose hearts are overflowing when they first hold their children in their arms, don't want to provide them with precisely that?

Yet the stress of life, our egoism, and our weakness often lead us to sin against that first love. And the culture of death frequently blinds us to what constitutes certain abuses. Interestingly, Karol Wojtyła—the future Pope John Paul II—pointed out in *Love and Responsibility* that another opposite of love (other than hatred) is using the other.[7] Instrumentalizing another for my needs goes against love and against the dignity of the other person, for it means turning them into a means. And as the philosopher Immanuel Kant already stated, the person may never be

---

[7] Karol Wojtyła, *Love and Responsibility*, trans. H. T. Willetts (San Francisco, CA: Ignatius Press, 1993), p. 28.

used as the means to an end, but is always an end in their own right. Therefore, if I use another person for my sexual satisfaction, as an emotional crutch, or merely as a way of fulfilling my various needs, then I am objectifying them, going against their intrinsic dignity, sinning against them, and potentially wounding them deeply. This instrumentalizing can happen in any kind of relationship, be it between spouses, parents and children, or friends, for example. This is not to say that it would be wrong for the other to fulfill my various needs, but this is a gift arising from the context of mutual love and self-gift and should not be the purpose or "theme" of the relationship.

GOD'S SUPERNATURAL PLAN

Gift of self is therefore the universal calling of all human beings, whatever their situation, talents, sufferings, and challenges. However, the way it expresses itself depends on the particular situation, personality, and vocation of each person. It is particularly frustrating, if spouses cannot experience the specific fruitfulness tied to their state of having children. Analogously, a diocesan priest would probably suffer from being prevented from celebrating the sacraments for the faithful or giving any pastoral care.

But God still has an amazing plan for all those suffering, for those whose life seems to make little sense when human happiness appears to have become impossible in their eyes. From a natural perspective, suffering seems meaningless. But when God allows us to be broken, then He is calling us to something greater, as will hopefully become clearer in the last chapter. The relationship between the spouses may be strained, perhaps even to its breaking point or beyond, because of the heavy cross of infertility. But the call to fruitfulness in their marriage remains.

In contrast to priests and religious, spouses suffering from infertility haven't chosen to forego having biological children. Instead, they are being denied the visible fruit of their vocation and the parenting which is normally part of it. It can be jarring to them, therefore, when the spiritual fruitfulness of celibate saints is brought to their attention; for they did not choose it like the latter and spiritual fruitfulness can seem like a distant and meager consolation for an empty cradle. However, spiritual fecundity is something we are all called to, whatever our state in life; therefore, we can learn from celibate and married saints, even if the nature of our crosses may differ.

St. Thérèse of Lisieux, who was hidden away in Carmel for nine years, comes to mind. Thousands of conversions and miracles have been attributed to her; her writings have been translated into more than fifty languages, and millions of copies have been published throughout the world.[8] The "science of love" she developed has afforded her the title of doctor of the Church. She who would have loved to be a missionary has become the patron saint of missions. God honored her missionary zeal by giving her posthumously a worldwide evangelizing success which few others have reached during their life. It is hard to equal her in terms of spiritual fruitfulness; she must be surrounded by so many people in heaven who have grown, nay, even been saved through her help. Their relationship is one of children to their mother—no less real than here on earth, but much closer and more perfect. The deep love and joy they experience through this bond must be tremendous.

In Thérèse's case, God lifted the veil at least partially after her death to show her spiritual significance in salvation history.

---

[8] *"Histoire d'une âme (Thérèse de Lisieux),"* Wikipédia, Wikimedia Foundation, accessed September 6, 2021, https://fr.wikipedia.org/wiki/Histoire_d%27une_%C3%A2me_(Th%C3%A9r%C3%A8se_de_Lisieux).

But there are many who both live and die in a hidden way, their sanctity unknown even to those close to them. Their fruitfulness will only be known in the next life. Yet they will experience a joy so great that it surpasses anything they could ever have imagined. God will give recompense abundantly to those suffering from biological infertility, who live their lives nonetheless as a gift of self.

Because her love was so great, St. Thérèse would have liked to be an apostle or a missionary and go through all possible martyrdoms on earth. But then, reading St. Paul, she understood that the greatest of all vocations was love, and that by embracing her vocation of a hidden love, she would find herself at the very center of the Church. This is what she writes:

> I understood that the Church had a Heart and that this Heart was BURNING WITH LOVE. I understood it was Love alone that made the Church's members act, that if Love ever became extinct, apostles would not preach the Gospel and martyrs would not shed their blood. I understood that LOVE COMPRISED ALL VOCATIONS, THAT LOVE WAS EVERYTHING, THAT IT EMBRACED ALL TIMES AND PLACES. . . . IN A WORD, THAT IT WAS ETERNAL!

> Then, in the excess of my delirious joy, I cried out: O Jesus, my Love. . . . my vocation, at last I have found it. . . . MY VOCATION IS LOVE!

> Yes, I have found my place in the Church and it is You, O my God, who have given me this place; in the heart of

the Church, my Mother, I shall be Love. Thus I shall be everything, and thus my dream will be realized.[9]

Though we may not feel capable of reaching the spiritual heights of St. Thérèse of Lisieux, her "little way," which consists of abandoning ourselves to God in our very weakness, is at the reach of everyone. The detachment she reaches (from her own desire of being a missionary) may still seem unattainable to us who at the moment are so desperate to have a child. But this is because we still have much mourning to do. We'd like to skip over that part in order to experience the peace and joy of the saints, but we forget that they too suffered greatly. Rome was not built in a day, nor can we expect to achieve detachment and receive consolation quickly (this again will be discussed in greater detail in the last chapter). The main point here is that our fruitfulness will be real and have tremendous impact if we entrust our infertility to God. We will hopefully still experience the joy of bearing children ourselves, but in the meantime, we will have given God the possibility to act in our lives in ways that will amaze us.

The Jewish convert, Roy Schoeman, who was an agnostic at the time, writes about his mystical experience during which he "fell into Heaven." He experienced God's love in an overwhelming manner. At the same time, he saw his life through the eyes of God and realized that the times he had deemed disastrous were really moments of grace. This is what he writes:

> It is as though I "fell into Heaven." Everything changed
> from one moment to the next, but in such a smooth and

---

[9] "Ms B 03v," Archives du Carmel de Lisieux, Carmel de Lisieux, accessed September 6, 2021, https://www.archives-carmel-lisieux.fr/english/carmel/index.php/b03/b03v.

subtle way that I was not aware of any discontinuity. I felt myself in the immediate presence of God. I was aware of His infinite exaltedness, and of His infinite and personal love for me. I saw my life as though I was looking back on it after death, in His presence, and could see everything which I would be happy about and everything which I would wish I had done differently. I saw that every action I had ever done mattered, for good or for evil. I saw that everything which had ever happened in my life had been perfectly designed for my own good from the infinitely wise and loving hand of God, *not only including but especially those things which I at the time I* [sic] *thought had been the greatest catastrophes.*[10]

Though we may never have this kind of experience during our lifetime, God has given us people like Roy to tell us about what happened to them. This is an encouragement to continue, even if it feels like we are stumbling and falling more than walking. The periods of excruciating pain where our life seems on hold and useless may turn out to be the most precious times in our life.

TRUSTING GOD AND THE CHURCH

Frequently, we lack trust in God. Yes, as believers, we put our faith in Him, but it must leaven through all the different layers of our

---

[10] Roy Schoeman, "Roy Schoeman's Conversion Story," accessed September 6, 2021, Catholic Education Resource Center, https://www.catholic education.org/en/faith-and-character/faith-and-character/roy-schoeman-s -conversion-story.html, emphasis mine. Roy Schoeman is the author of *Salvation is from the Jews* (San Francisco, CA: Ignatius Press, 2004) and *Honey from the Rock* (San Francisco, CA: Ignatius Press, 2007).

being. Often, we tend to hold back certain areas of our life out of fear that God may ask for a painful transformation. But worse than that, we have a lurking suspicion instilled by the deceiver that God is cruel and wants our unhappiness. Already in Genesis, the serpent insidiously suggests to Eve that God is a tyrant, since He's forbidden them access to the tree for fear they might become like gods; the devil also implies that He is a liar, for contrary to what He has told them—he claims—they will not die from eating the fruit.[11] Once Adam and Eve have eaten of the fruit, the consequences are immediate. They hide from God and no longer perceive Him as their loving father. It will take a long preparation through salvation history and Christ's Incarnation to the full revelation that we are truly His children and that no hair falls off our heads without Him knowing it.[12]

Christ has founded the Church and entrusted it with the power to maintain, develop, and explain His doctrine. She is His beloved Bride for whom He has given His life. Whatever the sinfulness of individual clergymen or laypeople (and ourselves) may be, this does not affect the holiness nor the mission of the Church. Though decisions made by the hierarchy may be wrong, the *depositum fidei* will never be lost.

This is something I believe we need to keep in mind when

---

[11] Pope John Paul II, *Man and Woman He Created Them*, 26:4 (pp. 236–237).

[12] Pope John Paul II, *Man and Woman He Created Them*, 27:1–2 (pp. 238–239). After the Fall, "man [is] deprived of participation in the Gift, man [is] alienated from the Love that was the source of the original gift, the source of the fullness of good intended for the creature." Fr. Jean C. J. d'Elbée, in his wonderful book *I Believe in Love*, 2nd ed., trans. Marilyn Teichert and Madeleine Stebbins (Manchester, NH: Sophia Institute Press, 2001), gives good suggestions as to how to obtain that trust as well as Jacques Philippe in his fantastic book *Searching for and Maintaining Peace: A Small Treatise on Peace of Heart*, trans. George and Jannie Driscoll (Staten Island, NY: St. Paul's, 2002).

dealing with certain Church teachings that we may not want to hear. Though they may go against our present wishes, they are not there to make life difficult but to protect us from paths that lead to sin and therefore to much hurt, even if this is not immediately evident to us.

With this in mind, I will now turn in the next chapter to various treatment options, looking at them both from the perspective of the Church, our Mother who wants to protect her children from the wounds of sin, and from a scientific point of view. The goal of any treatment should be to find true healing using methods that do not injure the human person's dignity at any point.

Chapter 5

TREATING INFERTILITY: ASSISTED REPRODUCTIVE TECHNOLOGIES (ART) VERSUS NAPROTECHNOLOGY

L et us now turn to the options offered to couples suffering from infertility these days. After having surmounted denial (if present), the couple is ready to look at the possible solutions to their problem. The hope and goal, after all, is to find healing, not to accept fatalistically an infertility that could be overcome. *In vitro* fertilization (or IVF) in various forms is generally suggested to them (artificial insemination is less in use).[1] Even couples

---

[1] In the USA, for example, in 2018 alone, according to the American Society for Reproductive Medicine, 74,590 babies were born as a result of IVF, which is almost 2% of the babies born that year; "More than 77 Thousand Babies Born from ART," ASRM, March 26, 2021, accessed October 26, 2021, https://www.asrm.org/news-and-publications/news-and-research/press

who have not fully explored the reasons for their infertility yet are encouraged to undergo IVF—in part because it is very lucrative for the health professionals involved. There are, however, much more promising treatment options.

For IVF turns out to be a poisoned chalice. As I intend to show by drawing on the Church's teaching, it affects marriage in its core and contradicts the precious dignity of the child, sometimes causing great hurt. Furthermore, it is far from certain that it will yield the much longed-for child in the end. The number of children born through IVF is fairly low because of a high failure rate. In the United States, there is only a 36% chance of having a baby in one's arms by the end of the grueling procedures. Also, its potential negative effects, be they physiological or psychological, on the children, the woman, and the couple are serious.

Though IVF permits some couples to conceive without too many difficulties or traumas, others will carry scars for the rest of their lives. In any case, it is important at the very least to measure the risks and to be aware of the ethical reasons against it.

In this chapter, I will attempt to show why these options are really siren songs leading down a path of hurt and grief, though that may not be immediately apparent. The Church forbids these techniques because they go against the laws of love and not—as some might wrongly think—because they are artificial. Let us therefore take a look at some empirical data in light of Catholic doctrine.

-releases-and-bulletins/more-than-77-thousand-babies-born-from-ART/. Between 1987 and 2015, 1 million babies were born in the US through the use of IVF or other reproductive technologies; "IVF by the Numbers," Penn Medicine, University of Pennsylvania, March 14, 2018, accessed September 5, 2021, https://www.pennmedicine.org/updates/blogs/fertility-blog/2018/march/ivf-by-the-numbers.

This chapter is heavy on science and draws on studies to give data and stats. It is certainly different in tone and approach from the previous chapters. Readers who are not interested in this information can easily move on to the next chapter.

By the way, though the content is scientific, I intentionally talk about "children" and "babies" when referring to the embryos created through IVF. Though the medical terms "zygotes," "blastocysts," "embryos," and "fetuses," are simply meant to refer to different stages of development of the human being before birth, they have the unfortunate connotation and effect of making the unborn seem less human. Treating them therefore with less than absolute respect seems easier if talking about them in these scientific terms. But when a woman is pregnant, she will always say that she is expecting a baby or a child, not an embryo or a fetus. My intention is to emphasize the reality of the full humanity and personhood of children from conception, hence my choice of words.

THE PROCEDURE: RISKS AND COSTS

I will start by explaining the procedure and its implications. Initially, having an *in vitro* child was presented as an exception that would rarely be used. The first test-tube baby, Louise Brown, was born in 1978 after many failed attempts. Since then, IVF has become an increasingly common procedure.

According to the CDC, there were 306,197 cycles of IVF performed in 456 reporting clinics in the United States in 2018. From 103,078 of these cycles, all embryos and eggs were frozen for future use. From the others came 73,831 live births, which means a 36% success rate per cycle, which is pretty good compared to the past; others estimate a lower success rate.[2] But in any case, the other 64% end up without a child after having gone through a grueling process and are left with a number of emotional and other scars.[3]

THE RISKS AND COSTS

Though 36% may seem promising enough to couples desperate for a child, they should keep in mind that never in the history of medicine has a medical breakthrough cost so many lives. The contempt with which human embryos are thrown away, subjected to quality control, and delivered for systematic vivisection is unparalleled in the history of the world. Until recently—looking at the success rate per child—only 8%–10% of all babies engendered through IVF were born; 90% died.[4] With the current 36% success rate of live births per cycle, however, the success rate increases slightly, namely between 12% and 18% per inserted child, depending on whether two or three were used. But this still means that 82%–88% of children engendered through IVF die in the process.

---

[2] "ART Success Rates," National Center for Chronic Disease Prevention and Health Promotion, CDC, accessed January 2, 2021, https://www.cdc.gov/art/artdata/index.html; "IVF by the Numbers."

[3] The CDC website states that "although the use of ART is still relatively rare as compared to the potential demand, its use has almost doubled over the past decade. Approximately 1.9% of all infants born in the United States every year are conceived using ART." "ART Success Rates."

[4] Fertility clinics prefer to look at the success rate per cycle rather than per implanted embryo because it appears more promising and hides the procedure's high death rate. It is interesting to note that some years ago in Victoria, Australia, where comprehensive data are legally required to be published, almost 98% of embryos were shown not to survive (John I. Fleming, *Dignitas Personae Explained: The Catholic Church's Teaching on Reproductive and Related Technologies*, Living Ethics Series (Ballan, Australia: Modotti Press, 2010), p. 37.

In 2018, it was estimated that 8 million babies had been born through IVF in the world, which means that about 72 million children died in the process (counting a 10% chance of survival by child—not per cycle).[5] This is hard to fathom! Any other medical procedure with this failure rate would not be allowed. Yet one of the inventors of IVF, Dr. Robert Edwards, received the Nobel Prize for Medicine or Physiology in 2010.

As Cardinal William Levada wrote pertinently in the Congregation for the Doctrine of the Faith's instruction *Dignitas Personae*:

> One is struck by the fact that, in any other area of medicine, ordinary professional ethics and the healthcare authorities themselves would never allow a medical procedure which involved such a high number of failures and fatalities. In fact, techniques of *in vitro* fertilization are accepted based on the presupposition that the individual embryo is not deserving of full respect in the presence of the competing desire for offspring which must be satisfied.[6]

---

[5] "More than 8 Million Babies Born from IVF since the World's First in 1978," European Society of Human Reproduction and Embryology, ScienceDaily, July 3, 2018, https://www.sciencedaily.com/releases/2018/07/180703084127.htm.

[6] Congregation for the Doctrine of the Faith, Instruction on Certain Bioethical Questions *Dignitas Personae* (December 8, 2008), § 15 (hereafter cited in text as DP). A bit earlier in the same document it says: "It is true that approximately a third of women who have recourse to artificial procreation succeed in having a baby. It should be recognized, however, that given the proportion between the total number of embryos produced and those eventually born, *the number of embryos sacrificed is extremely high.* These losses are accepted by the practitioners of *in vitro* fertilization as the price to be paid for positive results. In reality, it is deeply disturbing that research in this

If medicine does not allow for such a high rate of fatalities in any other area, one must ask oneself why this is the case here. One reason is certainly the highly lucrative nature of the business. The IVF revenue in the United States was estimated at $4.9 billion in 2020. The average cycle costs between $10,000 and $15,000.[7]

But let us look more closely at the procedure now.

The Procedure

The eggs are procured by using hyper-ovulatory drugs on the woman. These can cause Ovarian Hyper-Stimulation Syndrome (OHSS) and in extreme cases can even lead to death.[8] The ovaries fill with fluid; if this fluid retention becomes problematic, it may leak into cavities of the body such as the chest. Renal failure, thrombosis, internal hemorrhaging from ovarian rupture, as well as severe respiratory distress can, in rare cases, lead to death while in its mild forms the woman experiences nausea, bloating, and weight-gain, among other negative side effects.

But even for the man, the procurement of gametes is

area aims principally at obtaining better results in terms of the percentage of babies born to women who begin the process, but does not manifest a concrete interest in the right to life of each individual embryo" (DP 14).

[7] Ravi Telugunta, Smita Nerkar, and Onkar Sumant, "U.S. IVF Services Market by Cycle Type (Fresh IVF Cycle, Thawed IVF Cycle and Donor Egg IVF Cycle) and End User (Fertility Clinics, Hospitals, Surgical Centers, and Clinical Research Institutes): Analysis and Industry Forecast, 2019–2027," U.S. IVF Services Market, Allied Market Research, June 2020, https://www.alliedmarketresearch.com/US-IVF-services-market, "IVF by the Numbers."

[8] One woman in 400,000 to 500,000 are at risk of dying; see Klaus Fiedler and Diego Ezcurra, "Predicting and Preventing Ovarian Hyperstimulation Syndrome (OHSS): the Need for Individualized not Standardized Treatment," Reproductive Biology and Endocrinology, National Center for Biotechnology Information, April 24, 2012, https://www.ncbi.nlm.nih.gov/pmc/articles/PMC3403873/.

unpleasant; couples have said how disagreeable and artificial an experience it is (apart from the moral ramifications) to masturbate in a room where the man is either given pornographic material or where he can download his own. This is certainly not a loving context for a baby to come into being; the man and woman do not come together in an act of love, but become merely providers of the "parts" required to produce the baby. This denigrates them and goes against the high calling of medicine, as enunciated in *Donum Vitae*: "The humanization of medicine, which is insisted upon today by everyone, requires respect for the integral dignity of the human person first of all in the act and at the moment in which the spouses transmit life to a new person" (DV chap. 2, § 7).

In these circumstances, the man is unfaithful to his spouse, since he uses his sexuality for other purposes than showing his love to her. By watching porn, he degrades himself as well as the women on the porn sites, even if they should happen to sell themselves of their own free will. This is a dangerous path that can quickly lead to addiction.[9]

Once the doctors have chosen the gametes, the latter are then placed in petri dishes in a nutrient-rich serum, where conception takes place. Sometimes they proceed with an Intracytoplasmic

---

[9] Hospitals support the pornographic industry by buying these kinds of magazines or videos, which is unacceptable; see Michael Cook, "Ban Pornography in UK IVF Clinics, Says Think Tank," *BioEdge*, September 25, 2010, www.bioedge.org/index.php/bioethics/bioethics_article/ban_pornography_in_uk_ivf_clinics_says_think_tank; Rob Pollack, "Medicinal Masturbation: The Man's Role in IVF," *Elephant Journal*, January 8, 2013, www.elephantjournal.com/2013/01/medicinal-masturbation-the-mans-role-in-ivf-rob-pollak/. Here's a more recent article on men's personal experience: Unity Blott, "'I had a TV and very bushy German porn': Sperm Donors Reveal What It's REALLY Like Inside a Collection Room," *Daily Mail*, June 30, 2016, https://www.dailymail.co.uk/femail/article-3666049/Sperm-donors-reveal-s-REALLY-inside-collection-room-reddit.html.

Sperm Injection (ICSI), injecting one sperm cell directly into the egg (I will speak about this method later). The embryos are monitored, and only the healthiest are placed in the uterus, while the remaining ones are discarded, used for experiments, or frozen in liquid nitrogen for future use. But this is just the beginning of the problems, choices, and heartaches that the couple now has to face.

Frozen Embryos

Couples need to decide what to do with their remaining frozen embryos, which is for many a difficult and heart-wrenching process. They have the option of keeping them for future use (though they have to pay for storage), to have them discarded, to give them up for scientific research, or to donate them to another infertile couple for adoption. Some don't answer the fertility clinic's queries, move away, or separate—and the clinic loses track of them. In a fertility clinic in Fort Myers, Florida, 18% of frozen embryos have been abandoned, though the average seems to be closer to 5%–7%.[10] There are estimates that 1.4 million embryos are frozen in the United States, though others give lower estimates of a few hundred thousand.[11]

---

[10] Marilynn Marchione, "In Limbo: Leftover Embyos Challenge Clinics, Couples," Medical Xpress, Science X Network, January 17, 2019, https://medicalxpress.com/news/2019-01-limbo-leftover-embryos-clinics-couples.html.

[11] Bianca Bagnarelli, "Nation's Fertility Clinics Struggle with a Growing Number of Abandoned Embyos," NBC News, NBC Universal, August 12, 2019, https://www.nbcnews.com/health/features/nation-s-fertility-clinics-struggle-growing-number-abandoned-embryos-n1040806. Given that in France alone there were 221,538 frozen embryos in 2015, of whom 30,000 had been abandoned, it makes sense to give credence to the much higher estimates for the United States.

By the end of 2015, according to the register of the *Agence de biomédecine*,

This terrible situation of hundreds of thousands of embryos being frozen in a suspended state—some abandoned, others given up for research, and only some given to other infertile couples— shows the contradiction inherent in this technique. In order to have a child or children at all costs, one is willing to sacrifice others. This is the consequence of a utilitarian approach, of using another, which is the opposite of love, as shown in the previous chapter. As Cardinal Levada says so rightly in the instruction *Dignitas Personae*:

> All things considered, it needs to be recognized that the thousands of abandoned embryos represent a *situation of injustice which in fact cannot be resolved*. Therefore, John Paul II made an "appeal to the conscience of the world's scientific authorities and in particular to doctors, that the production of human embryos be halted, taking into account that there seems to be no morally licit solution regarding the human destiny of the thousands and thousands of 'frozen' embryos which are and remain the subjects of essential rights and should therefore be protected by law as human persons." (DP 19)[12]

221,538 embryos were frozen in France; see the article "Devenir des embryons congelés en France," by Oxana Blagosklonov and Céline Bruno, *La Revue du Practicien*, September 2018, https://www.larevuedupraticien.fr/article/de venir-des-embryons-congeles-en-france, originally published in in *La Revue du practicien* 68, no. 7 (2018): p. 713.

[12] Referencing Pope John Paul II, Address to the Participants in the Symposium on "*Evangelium vitae* and Law" and the Eleventh International Colloquium on Roman and Canon Law (May 24, 1996). The first embryo adoption service was started by the Christian adoption service Nightlight, which launched the Snowflakes Frozen Embryo Adoption and Donation Program in 1997, found at https://nightlight.org/snowflakes-embryo-adoption-donation /embryo-adoption/why-choose-snowflakes/. However admirable it is to want

MISCARRIAGE

Another risk of *in vitro* is a higher percentage of miscarriages, somewhere between 20% and 34%.[13] After experiencing many years of infertility, it is even more heart-wrenching to experience the death of a child (however early in the pregnancy that may be) whom one desired so intensely.

Since the risk of miscarriage is strong, more than one embryo is normally transferred into the woman's uterus. If the couples in question are not ready to have twins or triplets, they then have recourse to abortion, euphemistically called "embryonic reduction." How ironic! These couples who have been wanting children for years are killing those they consider to be too many, which again underlines the utilitarian nature of the procedure.

In countries like France, the number of embryos implanted is limited to three per cycle. But this is not the case in the United States, where IVF is not well regulated. Though the case of Nadya Suleman in California, who gave birth to octuplets in 2009 despite the fact that she already had other children and no partner, was exceptional, it shows the inherent dangers of the procedure.[14] This situation was surely not good for the mother nor the children when nature would generally prevent something like this from happening.

---

to help frozen embryos, the problem with embryo adoption, as will become clear, is in many ways the same as with surrogacy or donor children. The only ones who may have already existing frozen embryos implanted are the biological parents.

[13] Alastair G. Sutcliffe and Michael Ludwig, "Outcome of Assisted Reproduction," *Lancet*, 370 (9584) (2007): pp. 351–359, p. 352. I am assuming Sutcliffe and Ludwig are counting as miscarriage only those cases where embryos have implanted, but then do not survive. Otherwise, one would have to count the 80%–90% of embryos that either don't implant or don't make it to term.

[14] "Suleman Octuplets," Wikipedia, Wikimedia Foundation, accessed March 1, 2021, https://en.wikipedia.org/wiki/Suleman_octuplets.

Preimplantation Genetic Diagnosis (PGD or PIGD)

Sometime between the third and the fifth day, once the embryos have already gone through many cell divisions (20–200), a choice has to be made concerning which ones should be implanted in the woman. They are screened for genetic abnormalities or conditions that may lead to diseases later on, and only the healthiest ones are implanted. This is clearly a form of eugenics and discriminates against people with disabilities, whether born or unborn. In the United States, it is a standard practice and not regulated by law.[15]

Dignitas Personae (quoting *Evangelium Vitae*), therefore rightly states:

> Preimplantation diagnosis is therefore the expression of a *eugenic mentality* that "accepts selective abortion in order to prevent the birth of children affected by various types of anomalies. Such an attitude is shameful and utterly reprehensible, since it presumes to measure the value of a human life only within the parameters of 'normality' and physical well-being, thus opening the way to legitimizing infanticide and euthanasia as well." (DP 22)[16]

Leaving one's children at the mercy of technicians who decide which child should live and which one shouldn't means putting one's children at risk in an unacceptable manner. For it "establishes

---

[15] See Michelle J. Bayevsky, "Comparative Preimplantation Genetic Diagnosis Policy in Europe and the USA and Its Implications for Reproductive Tourism," *Reproductive Biomedicine and Society Online* 3 (December 2016): pp. 41–47, https://doi.org/10.1016/j.rbms.2017.01.001.

[16] Quoting Pope John Paul II, Encyclical on the Value and Inviolability of Human Life *Evangelium Vitae* (March 25, 1995), § 63 (hereafter cited in text as EV).

the domination of technology over the origin and destiny of the human person," to quote from *Donum Vitae*. "Such a relationship of domination is in itself contrary to the dignity and equality that must be common to parents and children" (DV chap. 2, § 5).

Donor Parents and Surrogacy

Doctors suggest that when either or both spouses have medical problems that render them incapable or make it inadvisable for them to have their own biological children, the egg, sperm, or both are taken from donors for IVF (the gametes are then said to be heterologous, rather than homologous, i.e., from the parents). This raises the question of who the real mother or father of the child is. Is it the egg donor, the sperm donor, or perhaps the surrogate mother carrying the baby to term, or is it the parent or parents raising the child? This has led to the strange distinction between biological and social parents. Since there are no federal laws regarding these questions in the United States, in contrast to many countries in Europe, couples are encouraged to draw up contracts to avoid difficulties. However, there is no watertight solution. The legal problems involved in this quagmire seem minor compared to the pain and abandonment the child might experience.

JayCee Buzzanca from California came into existence through a donor egg and a donor sperm and a surrogate mother. When the couple who commissioned her separated, the husband claimed he didn't have to pay child support since the child was not his. The judge ruled in favor of Mr. Buzzanca but also stated that Mrs. Buzzanca was not JayCee's mother either. JayCee found herself legally fatherless and motherless while the social mother and father, the surrogate mother, the egg donor, and sperm donor were battling over custody.[17]

Or what happens when a surrogate mother and the commissioning couple are in disagreement? What if the surrogate mother does not want to give up the child or the commissioning couple gets a divorce and is no longer interested in having the yet-to-be-born child? Or what if the biological parent of some frozen embryos dies, as in the case of Julie Garber?[18] Do the inheritors, such as Garber's parents, become the "owners" of those embryos? Who is to decide what becomes of them? Or what if the unborn child turns out to be disabled? In one such case, the commissioning couple wanted the surrogate mother to abort the child; though she refused at first, she was later persuaded that it was not "her" abortion but theirs.[19] In other cases, the surrogate mother refused and kept the baby herself.[20]

The number of sperm donations is not recorded nor limited in the United States. In 1988, the Office of Technology Assessment suggested there were 30,000 sperm donations per year. This estimate has been used over the last thirty years and is the basis for what is now an updated number of 60,000 per year. However,

---

[17] "A High-Tech Orphan," CBS News, ViacomCBS, May 13, 1998, https://www.cbsnews.com/news/a-high-tech-orphan/; Peter Garrett, "Endgame: Reproductive Technology & The Death of Natural Procreation" (lecture, National Life Conference, Leamington, Canada, 1999); see also Rick Weiss, "Babies in Limbo: Laws Outpaced by Fertility Advances," *The Washington Post*, February 8, 1998, http://www.washingtonpost.com/wp-srv/national/science/ethical/fertility1.htm.

[18] Weiss, "Babies in Limbo."

[19] See Garrett, "Endgame."

[20] Nicole Pelletiere, "Surrogate Mother Who Kept Baby with Down Syndrome Says Toddler Is Hitting Milestones," yahoo!news, Yahoo, April 19, 2016, https://www.yahoo.com/gma/surrogate-mom-kept-baby-down-syndrome-says-toddler-110959987--abc-news-parenting.html.

the original number was only a guess in the first place and is likely a gross underestimation. The American Society for Reproductive Medicine's guidelines advise no more than 25 pregnancies per donor per 800,000 people.[21] This means that a donor's sperm can be used again for each new set of 800,000 people. If one does the math, as Wendy Kramer from the Donor Siblings Registry did, that would mean 255 pregnancies per donor for the city of New York and, crazily, 213,766 for the world population. Though no one is aiming for that, it shows that these non-binding guidelines are anything but sufficient.[22]

Given that there is no central registry and that fertility clinics are not necessarily following the number of children born from donations, the potential for abuse is great. Some men make sperm donations in several states. And it is not unusual anymore for donor-conceived children to have fifty half-siblings or more. When Cynthia Daily and her partner decided to have a child through sperm donation in 2004, she could not have imagined that seven years later their son would have 149 half-siblings with the possibility of more.[23]

Egg donations are less frequent, since the harvesting is more difficult and problematic for the women. But these donations

---

[21] Practice Committee of the American Society for Reproductive Medicine and Practice Committee of the Society for Assisted Reproductive Technology, "Repetitive Oocyte Donation: A Committee Opinion," *Fertility and Sterility* 113, no. 6 (June 2020): pp. 1150–1152, accessed at https://www.asrm.org /globalassets/asrm/asrm-content/news-and-publications/practice-guidelines /for-non-members/repetitive_oocyte_donation.pdf.

[22] Wendy Kramer, "How Many Donor Offspring Are Really Out There?," The Donor Sibling Registry, December 23, 2013, https://www.donorsibling registry.com/blog/how-many-donor-offspring-are-really-out-there/.

[23] Jacqueline Mroz, "One Sperm Donor, 150 Offspring," *The New York Times*, September 5, 2011, https://www.nytimes.com/2011/09/06/health/06donor .html.

are worse in a certain sense, since another level of exploitation is reached. The eggs are generally acquired from women who are financially vulnerable and who sell their bodies to improve their living conditions. Fertility clinics frequently use altruistic language in their ads searching for remunerated egg donors.[24] However, no desire to assist someone else ever justifies allowing oneself to be used. These gamete donations may well haunt the donors later in life, be it for legal, emotional, or moral reasons. The telling documentary *Eggsploitation*, by Jennifer Lahl and the Center for Bioethics and Culture Network, reveals the nasty side of the industry, showing young women whose health and fertility have been lastingly compromised.

The fact that eggs are harvested from women, whether for donation or not, reduces women to their reproductive capacities, something that should set off feminist alarm bells. The term "harvest" already expresses this instrumentalization. Instead of being a mother, who conceives and bears her child, the woman simply contributes her eggs. Some feminists are therefore speaking out against reproductive technologies, as, for example, in a document put together by the Feminist International Network of Resistance to Reproductive and Genetic Engineering. In their eyes, reproduction, which was a woman's domain until recently, has now been given over to men. The new medical technocracy does not give infertile women control over their fertility as the healing of their condition would, but simply hands it over to the

---

[24] E. Christian Brugger, writes in his article for *Zenit*, "The Incredible, Profitable Egg: 'Eggsploitation' Uncovers Dark Side of Infertility Industry," about the industrialized exploitation of women for their eggs with potentially dire consequences for their health, October 8, 2010, https://www.ewtn.com/catholicism/library/incredible-profitable-egg-9724.

medical profession.[25] Technicians now bring about life. Given that reproductive technologies almost always involve eugenic screening, this network of women also fears that pressure will be exercised to bring forth only perfect children, consequently straining the parent-child relationship. And if they refuse screening and their child has health issues, they might be accused of child abuse.[26]

In March 2005, the European Parliament issued the European Parliament Resolution on the Trade in Human Egg Cells, condemning the trade of human eggs since "harvesting of egg cells poses a high medical risk to the life and health of women." And "despite the possibility of serious effects on women's life and health, the high price paid for egg cells incites and encourages donation, given the relative poverty of the donors." In her article "Egg Donors and Human Trafficking," Michele Clark therefore sees egg donation as a form of human trafficking.[27]

---

[25] This document is mentioned and some of its significant points are analyzed in Vincenza Mele and Anne Rita Morgani's article "The Feminist Voice on Reproductive Technologies," *Women's Health Issues*, ed. Antonio G. Spagnolo and Gabriella Gambino (Rome: Societa Editrice Universa, 2003), pp. 243–246. This network's principles and documents can be found at "FINRRAGE," accessed November 18, 2020, http://www.finrrage.org/. Obviously, a distinction needs to be made between those feminists who see their fertility itself as oppressive and as exploited by patriarchal dominion to keep them subjected and those feminists who, on the contrary, see this domain as their realm over which patriarchal power tries to get control through reproductive technologies. Therefore, Mele and Morgani distinguish between radical feminists who hold the first and cultural feminists who defend the second position.

[26] Mele and Morgani, "The Feminist Voice on Reproductive Technologies," pp. 244–245.

[27] The quotations from this paragraph come from Michele Clark, "Egg Donors and Human Trafficking," *First Things*, April 1, 2008, https://www.firstthings.com/web-exclusives/2008/04/egg-donors-and-human-trafficking.

Inbreeding

Since the identity of the egg and sperm donors have been kept anonymous in most countries until recently (and still are in the United States), inbreeding is a real possibility. Some men's sperm is used for the engendering of many babies because they fit the criteria many women seek. In Holland, with its low population of about 17 million, Louis (an alias) made sperm donations up to three times a week for decades. He claims he has 200 children, but other estimates speak of 1,000.[28] Or there is the famous example of the owner of a fertility clinic who may have fathered up to 600 children.[29] There are many more examples of this. It cannot but make donor children feel confused knowing they may have dozens or hundreds of siblings. Not surprisingly, donor children are therefore afraid of unknowingly falling in love with a relative, more so than those adopted (46% of donor children compared to 17% of adopted children).[30]

The children from donated gametes who find their donor parent will be faced with the fact that this parent himself does not know his family. These children will feel even more at a loss.[31]

[28] Simon Usborne, "'I thought—who will remember me?': The Man Who Fathered 200 Children," *The Guardian*, November 24, 2018, https://www.theguardian.com/science/2018/nov/24/sperm-donor-man-who-fathered-200-children.

[29] Rebecca Smith, "British Man 'Fathered 600 Children' at Own Fertility Clinic," *The Telegraph*, April 8, 2012, https://www.telegraph.co.uk/news/9193014/British-man-fathered-600-children-at-own-fertility-clinic.html.

[30] Elizabeth Marquardt, Norval D. Glenn, and Karen Clark, *My Daddy's Name Is Donor: A New Study of Young Adults Conceived through Sperm Donation* (New York: Institute for American Values, 2010), p. 35.

[31] Ibid. pp. 35–36. In the survey group, 20% of the adult donor children had already donated their sperm or eggs compared to 1% of people raised by their biological parents in the same group. Hence the potential confusion and risk of inbreeding rises exponentially over generations.

It is true that available widespread genetic testing like 23andMe and websites for donor children make it possible to find one's siblings—and if one is lucky, one's donor parent—but it is still unsettling. And it would make people fearful of falling in love before they are able to eliminate the possibility of being close family. What heartbreaks must ensue when they fall in love, only to find out that they are half-siblings! And when siblings have not grown up together, they are more likely to find each other sexually attractive, making the risk of incest rise.[32]

THE PSYCHOLOGICAL AND SPIRITUAL TRAUMA OF REPRODUCTIVE TECHNOLOGIES

But there are even further complications to take into consideration. In their study from 2010, *My Daddy's Name Is Donor*, Elizabeth Marquardt, Norval D. Glenn, and Karen Clark came up with the following findings:

> We learned that, on average, young adults conceived through sperm donation are hurting more, are more confused, and feel more isolated from their families. They fare worse than their peers raised by biological parents on important outcomes such as depression, delinquency, and substance abuse. Nearly two-thirds agree, "My sperm donor is half of who I am." Nearly half are disturbed that money was involved in their conception. More than half say that when they see someone who resembles them, they wonder if they are related. Almost as many say they have feared being attracted to or having sexual relations

---

[32] Ross Clark, "The Incest Trap."

with someone to whom they are unknowingly related. Approximately two-thirds affirm the right of donor offspring to know the truth about their origins. And about half of donor offspring have concerns about or serious objections to donor conception itself, even when parents tell their children the truth.[33]

Forty-five percent are bothered by the manner of their conception and almost half think of it a few times a week, if not more. Seventy percent wonder what their sperm donor family is like, and 69% ask themselves whether their sperm donor's parents, that is, their grandparents, wouldn't want to know them.[34] These percentages are much higher than those found in cases of adoption. Donor children also have much greater issues with trust, wondering whether their parents didn't lie to them while growing up.[35]

The Church defends the rights of children in her teaching, trying to prevent great sorrow and heartbreak. *Donum Vitae* states that "heterologous artificial fertilization violates the rights of the child; it deprives him of his filial relationship with his parental origins and can hinder the maturing of his personal identity" (DV chap. 2, § 2).

---

[33] Marquardt, Glenn, and Clark, *My Daddy's Name Is Donor*, pp. 5–6.

[34] Marquardt, Glenn, and Clark, *My Daddy's Name Is Donor*, pp. 7, 28.

[35] Marquardt, Glenn, and Clark, *My Daddy's Name Is Donor*, p. 8. Interestingly, though the percentage of donor children who are suffering from the manner of their conception is high (61%), they are still in favor of conception through donation; Marquardt, Glenn, and Clark, *My Daddy's Name Is Donor*, p. 13. However, this makes sense on a certain level; they may want to show solidarity to their social parents or recoil from taking a position that would imply that they should never have come into existence.

THE RIGHT TO KNOW ONE'S ORIGINS

About two-thirds of grown donor offspring think that they should get access to some information about their sperm donor (biological father), ranging from non-identifying data to knowing his identity, getting in touch with him, learning about the existence of half-siblings, and so forth.[36] Therefore Britain, Sweden, Norway, the Netherlands, Switzerland, Australia, and New Zealand have banned anonymous donation of sperm and eggs.[37] "A 2011 study in the journal *Human Reproduction*," as Ashley Fetters writes in her article "Finding the Lost Generation of Sperm Donors" in *The Atlantic*, "found that 82 percent of donor-conceived offspring hoped to make contact one day with their donor, most frequently because they were curious about their donor's physical appearance. A similar study found that 92 percent of the donor-conceived offspring surveyed were actively searching for their donor, their donor siblings, or both."[38]

Donor children are frequently traumatized because they have been instrumentalized and abandoned by their biological parents or parent. For example, donor-conceived Lynne Spencer states: "If

---

[36] In the 2020 survey of We Are Donor Conceived, the largest so far with 481 participants from 15 countries, 88% of donor-conceived people thought it a basic human right to know the identity of both biological parents. "10 Highlights from the 2020 We Are Donor Conceived Survey," We Are Donor Conceived, accessed September 7, 2021, https://www.wearedonorconceived.com/2020-survey-top/10-highlights-from-the-2020-we-are-donor-conceived-survey/.

[37] Marquardt, Glenn, and Clark, *My Daddy's Name Is Donor*, pp. 11–12; see also "Sperm Donation Laws by Country," Wikipedia, Wikimedia Foundation, accessed March 1, 2021, https://en.wikipedia.org/wiki/Sperm_donation_laws_by_country#Overview_table.

[38] Ashley Fetters, "Finding the Lost Generation of Sperm Donors," *The Atlantic*, May 18, 2018, https://www.theatlantic.com/family/archive/2018/05/sperm-donation-anonymous/560588/.

my life is for other people's purposes, and not my own, then what is the purpose of my life?"[39] Her existential experience reveals the terrible consequences of a utilitarian approach. If one is not loved for one's own sake, one loses one's sense of meaning; one feels lost.

This confirms the Church's teaching that "the child is not an object to which one has a right, nor can he be considered as an object of ownership: rather, a child is a gift, 'the supreme gift' and the most gratuitous gift of marriage, and is a living testimony of the mutual giving of his parents. For this reason, the child has the right . . . to be the fruit of the specific act of the conjugal love of his parents; and he also has the right to be respected as a person from the moment of his conception" (DV chap. 2, § 8). And as *Evangelium Vitae* rightly explains: "The meaning of life is found in giving and receiving love, and in this light human sexuality and procreation reach their true and full significance" (EV 81). One can easily lose sight of this meaning when one has been instrumentalized, even if only at conception.

To keep hidden from children that they have a donor parent or were engendered through IVF is not a good solution either. In that case, all clues and hints would have to be avoided; this makes for a strained atmosphere. Lynne Spencer again observes: "This need to hold back limits the level of emotional intimacy, openness, and honesty between people."[40] And Suzanne Ariel speaks from her own experience, when she says: "Living as a family with a terrible secret robs the family. It's a terrible, terrible thing to have happen. This rottenness just gets worse over the years."[41] Or Barry Stevens, who made the documentary *Offspring* on this issue,

---

[39] Marquardt, Glenn, and Clark, *My Daddy's Name Is Donor*, p. 24.
[40] Marquardt, Glenn, and Clark, *My Daddy's Name Is Donor*, p. 40.
[41] Marquardt, Glenn, and Clark, *My Daddy's Name Is Donor*, p. 51.

expresses himself this way: "The secret sits in the family like a little time bomb in the centre of things."[42] When there is an open family conflict, someone might suddenly reveal the truth. This comes as a great shock to the donor child while confirming some suspicions that something hadn't been quite right. Trust is undermined and already had been during the years of silence.[43]

Donum Vitae therefore rightly states:

> Heterologous artificial fertilization violates the rights of the child; it deprives him of his filial relationship with his parental origins and can hinder the maturing of his personal identity. Furthermore, it offends the common vocation of the spouses who are called to fatherhood and motherhood: it objectively deprives conjugal fruitfulness of its unity and integrity; it brings about and manifests a rupture between genetic parenthood, gestational parenthood and responsibility for upbringing. Such damage to the personal relationships within the family has repercussions on civil society: what threatens the unity and stability of the family is a source of dissension, disorder and injustice in the whole of social life. (DV chap. 2, § 2)

The mainstream approach among experts these days is to say that the problem lies with secrecy, not with the way donor children are conceived. However, in Marquardt's study only 29% of

---

[42] Marquardt, Glenn, and Clark, *My Daddy's Name Is Donor*, p. 51.

[43] Thus, it is not surprising that 47% of donor offspring compared to 27% among adopted children and 18% of those raised by their biological parents worry that their mother might have lied to them in important matters during their childhood. Concerning the father, the percentage is slightly lower with 43% versus 22% and 15%; Marquardt, Glenn, and Clark, *My Daddy's Name Is Donor*, pp. 51–52.

the children were told later in their teens or found out about their origins by chance. The remainder's parents were either very open about it from the beginning (59%) or they were told before the age of twelve. Yet 47% and 43% had trust issues regarding their mother and father respectively. This indicates that the issue isn't just the secrecy, but something about the procedure itself.[44] About 47% of donor children are concerned about the procedure or are against it (11%).[45]

The donor-conceived Lauren Burns' statement might shed some light on why some donor-conceived children do not seem affected by their conception: "Donor conceived children are generally smart and sensitive. They want to protect their parents. This often complicates the way they allow themselves to express their feelings about being donor conceived. They are generally especially sensitive about not upsetting the non-biological parent."[46] When they are young, these children will want to accept what their social parents have told them. It takes some distance and analysis to realize what might be bothering them deep down.

The suffering of donor-conceived children is real but often overlooked by society, which makes matters worse. Victims who are not heard suffer much more. Though they love the parents who raised them, they also seem to struggle with feelings of anger. As the website Them Before Us states, the fact that these donor-conceived children were intentionally denied a relationship with their biological parent(s) "often leads these kids to feel guilty,

---

[44] Marquardt, Glenn, and Clark, *My Daddy's Name Is Donor*, pp. 55–57.

[45] Marquardt, Glenn, and Clark, *My Daddy's Name Is Donor*, p. 57.

[46] Lauren Burns, "Lauren Burns 'Donor Conceived' Perspective," Donor Conceived Perspectives: Voices from the Offspring, February 4, 2010, http://donorconceived.blogspot.com/2010/02/lauren-burns-donor -conceived.html.

angry, ashamed and ... commodified." One donor-conceived adult woman, whose single mother desperately wanted a child, writes: "I love my mother but often I find myself despising her for doing this to me, for being so selfish. I, myself, as a woman approaching the big 3.5, I know what it feels like to truly want a child but NEVER would I knowingly take away a child's right to have a father and a family. Not only has my mother deprived me from having a father but also sisters, brothers, cousins, grandparents. . . ."[47] As Them Before Us points out, it is false to believe that "all kids need is love"; in reality, they also need to know of and have a relationship with their biological parents.

The Children Conceived through In Vitro and Educated by Their Biological Parents

The evidence we have indicating psychological as well as physical issues is worrying and should be taken seriously.[48] At the very least,

---

[47] "Biology Matters—Take it from Donor Conceived Kids with Loving Straight Parents," Them Before Us, September 14, 2017, https://thembeforeus.com/biology-matters-take-donor-conceived-kids-loving-straight-parents/.

[48] Not enough research has been made on the question whether IVF affects the physical and psychological health of children or not, and what has been done is still in the early phases. Therefore, one finds disagreement within the scientific community. The mainstream seems to think that there is no negative impact of IVF on children and that psychological issues are due to the parents' over-protectiveness caused by their long-lasting infertility rather than to the use of ART. Yet Dr. Alastair G. Sutcliffe, in his article "Reproductive Technology and Its Impact on Psychosocial Child Development" for the *Encyclopedia on Early Childhood Development*, in which he gives a survey on the studies in question, admits that there are some methodological issues; for example, studies generally only involve healthy children. If sick children are excluded from the investigation, then the studies must, by definition, be skewed. Furthermore, Sutcliffe concedes that one cannot determine whether the issues between parent and child are due to the procedure of IVF or to the long years of infertility. So how can one say for certain that the overprotectiveness

potential parents have a right to hear about the risks in order to give proper informed consent before making their decision about the use of reproductive technologies.

Today, prenatal experiences have been recognized as significant and constitutive for the child's psyche and health. Mothers speak and sing to their children in the womb, as do fathers. The fact that IVF children are engendered outside of the loving embrace of their parents in a sterile lab by technicians should therefore not be underestimated, even if it "merely" concerns the first three to five days of their life. Those children who are frozen before being implanted could potentially be even more traumatized, given their great vulnerability. Science, where it stands now, has no explanation for the following story, which is, however, no less real: The prenatal psychologist Karlton Terry describes a case in which a little girl conceived by IVF told her parents that she dreamt she had siblings—three sisters and four brothers—who were freezing in a cave, were crying, and needed to be saved. The parents confirmed that seven embryos remained frozen.[49] If children can be scarred because they lose a twin *in utero* dying of natural causes,

---

of the parents is the cause of the children's issues? November 2007, http://www.child-encyclopedia.com/documents/SutcliffeANGxp_rev.pdf.

[49] Karlton Terry, "Observations in Treatment of Children Conceived by In Vitro Fertilization," in *Ergebnisse der Pränatalen Psychologie*, ed. Ludwig Janus (Heidelberg, Germany: Mattes Verlag, 2004), p. 110. Though the girl mentioned three sisters and five brothers while there were only seven frozen embryos, the math is still correct, as Karlton Terry points out, since she has eight siblings, if one counts her born twin brother.

Karlton Terry also mentions the story of a one-year-old IVF twin who consistently looked up to her left while standing, having a very sad expression of intense longing on her face. He held various objects to the spot she was looking at, but only when he put two naked baby dolls, did she react strongly, tremble, cry, and run to her parents. Already before this experiment, the parents thought that she was looking for her frozen siblings, which the experiment seemed to confirm.

how much more will they be affected by the abortion of a sibling sharing the same space *in utero*, or by the discarding of their siblings during IVF?

Some psychologists speak therefore of survivor guilt, which is part of post-traumatic stress disorder, haunting abortion survivors. Children whose sibling(s) have been aborted, frozen, forgotten, or thrown away experience less trust, for the same could have happened to them. They carry a great weight and often feel that they have to prove themselves, to somehow justify their existence by being particularly successful—or on the contrary, give up even trying since they feel so overwhelmed.[50]

METHUSELAH'S DAUGHTERS

Another problematic aspect of IVF is that it allows increasingly older women to have children since there are no age limits in some countries. As an article from 2014 in the *Daily Mail* states, the number of women in their fifties having children had doubled over the previous five years in the United Kingdom; three children are born to mothers in their fifties every week in England, and the number of mothers younger than twenty-five has plummeted by half since the early 1970s.[51] Even women in their sixties

[50] See Philip Ney's article, "A Consideration of Abortion Survivors," about the psychological impact that abortion can have on the brothers and sisters of the aborted child. In *The Zero People: Essays on Life*, ed. Jeff Lane Hensely (Ann Arbor: Servant Books, 1983), pp. 123–138.

[51] Matt Chorley, "Birth to Mums over 50 Soaring: Midwives Raise Fears as Number Doubles in Five Years," *The Daily Mail*, March 30, 2014, http://www.dailymail.co.uk/news/article-2591736/Number-women-baby-turning-50-DOUBLES-just-five-years.html. Interestingly, the fertility experts attending the Pontifical Academy for Life's conference in the Vatican in 2012 agreed that most infertility could be avoided if people started having children in their twenties.

and seventies are giving birth due to reproductive technologies in India, Cyprus, or Ukraine. IVF-tourism makes it possible for the well-to-do—if they are lucky—to get their long-desired child, but again, often after much heartache and many unsuccessful attempts.

But what does it mean for a child to have a mother who could be her grandmother, leaving aside the medical problems, which the *Daily Mail* article mentions? In terms of energy levels, capacity to adapt, and bridging the generational gap, it is much better to be a younger rather than an older mother. Yes, there are problems too when parents are very young. Older mothers can be great caretakers and probably have more wisdom than younger ones. But are old mothers something we should strive for?

Young children whose mothers are in their sixties are much more likely to become orphans. If their mothers live into their own adulthood, then they will have to spend their early twenties taking care of their aging and dying parent(s). This is the time when they should go to college, have their first job, fall in love, and start their own family. Instead, they are housebound or at least greatly challenged with taking care of their old parent(s). If the generational order is respected, then generally one's parents need help when we, their children, are in our forties. At that point, we've probably established ourselves, our children are no longer small (or the older ones can help with the younger), and it is easier to take care of our parents.

If I look at the generational gap which existed between my grandmother and myself (though we both shared the faith and loved each other dearly), I would have found it very hard had she been my main caretaker. To know what is going on in current culture, to be able to talk to one's children about it, and to protect them means being engaged with it to a certain extent—something which decreases with age. Yes, there are exceptions; some mothers get children very late naturally and grandparents can be excellent caretakers of their grandchildren when the parents die young or can't do so themselves. If this can be achieved successfully, all the better. But desiring this to be a more widespread phenomenon means causing much grief to children.

Methuselah is mentioned for his old age in the Old Testament. For good reasons God didn't allow such longevity after the flood. Should we have our own female Methuselahs who have children in their old age? The same will happen to us as did to those who thought they could be like God by building the tower of Babel: confusion, mayhem, discord. I can only imagine the challenges for these children when noticing their mothers' old age, their having to take care of them early on, and wondering about their own origins, since they've probably been conceived through gamete donation.

Of course, there are biblical examples of old parents: Abraham and Sarah were over one hundred years old when they had Isaac, and Elizabeth had John the Baptist late in life. But these are exceptions, even miracles. Some women, it is true, can conceive naturally into their fifties, but this is rare. There is a reason why nature has set a limit to women's biological clock, painful as that is to those desperate to have children of their own.

The Physical Consequences of IVF

But there may also be negative physical consequences of IVF on the children. "Researchers at the University of Aarhus in Denmark found that babies born by IVF were more than twice as likely to have cerebral palsy as those conceived naturally," as a study published in *Human Reproduction* has shown.[52] According to Dr. Andrew Feinberg, professor of medicine at Johns Hopkins School of Medicine, a study funded by the National Institutes of Health indicated a worrying increase of Beckwith-Wiedemann syndrome. IVF children are six times more likely to have this syndrome, which expresses itself in a stiff and jerky gait, excessive laughter, seizures, and sometimes mental retardation and poor balance.[53]

The problems are accentuated, it seems, through Intracytoplasmic Sperm Injection (ICSI), where a single sperm is chosen and injected directly into the egg rather than letting the sperm penetrate the egg on its own in the petri dish. This procedure is generally used when the sperm is not sufficiently robust to fertilize an egg on its own. In the 2010 conference for the Advancing Science Service Society (ASSS), Professor Andre Van Steirteghem,

---

[52] Stephen Adams wrote about this study in his article "IVF 'Could Double Risk of Cerebral Palsy'" in *The Telegraph* on November 3, 2010, https://www.telegraph.co.uk/news/health/8104989/IVF-could-double-risk-of-cerebral-palsy.html. Interestingly, the study took into account the age and health of the mother; but all things being equal, IVF children were still twice as likely to suffer from cerebral palsy. In its issue from February 9, 2006, the medical journal *The Lancet* published a study done by the University Children's Hospital in Upsala, Sweden and found that "IVF-children were almost twice as likely to develop a neurological problem than those who were conceived naturally." According to the study, IVF children "were three times more likely to have cerebral palsy, and four times as likely to have some type of developmental delay." Bradley Mattes, "The Hidden Dangers of In Vitro Fertilization," Life Issues Institute, July 1, 2006, https://www.lifeissues.org/2006/07/hidden-dangers-vitro-fertilization/.

[53] "It [the syndrome] is characterized by an enlarged tongue, retardation, abnormalities in the kidney, liver, and spleen, and a predisposition for early childhood cancers. The research indicates that certain growth-regulating genes had a tendency to be imprinted incorrectly in babies conceived by IVF. Scientists called the link between Beckwith-Wiedemann and IVF 'strong.'" Mattes, "The Hidden Dangers of In Vitro Fertilization."

who developed the technique, warned that it "might enable fertilisation with genetically-defective sperm, raising the prospect that problems like diabetes, heart disease and obesity could be passed on to future generations" and should therefore only be used if conventional IVF does not work.[54] Other studies, showing that Beckwith-Wiedemann Syndrome and Angelman Syndrome occur more frequently, stated that "errors in the father's sperm may help to explain both the father's infertility and the origins of the condition in the affected child."[55] Thus, infertility could sometimes be nature's way of preventing grave illnesses from being passed on.

THE STRAIN ON MARRIAGE

But these are not the only dangers of reproductive technologies. Helen James's story, as she describes it in "IVF Destroyed My Family," is heartbreaking. She had one live-born child through IVF, but her marriage couldn't bear the strain of trying to have another child that way. She writes: "IVF technology and the hope it proffers has driven a stake through the very heart of my life. I have a son but I also have a divorce to my name, a string of lost or radically altered friendships, and the emotional scars of years of medical intervention. Society would call me churlish for saying it, because I got my 'prize,' but the relentless pursuit of fertility has been a poisoned chalice."[56]

---

[54] Summarized thus by Maren Urner in the article "IVF Technique is Overused, Says Its Inventor," *BioNews*, IVF.net, March 2, 2010, http://www.ivf.net/ivf/ivf-technique-is-overused-says-its-inventor-o4860.html.

[55] Urner, "IVF Technique is Overused, Says Its Inventor."

[56] Helen James, "'IVF destroyed my family': How a Mother's Desperate Quest for a Second Child Took Over Her Life," *The Daily Mail*, October 23, 2010, http://www.dailymail.co.uk/home/you/article-1321907/Helen-James-IVF-destroyed-family.html#ixzz14gZftHX8.

Helen James' first IVF pregnancy ended in a miscarriage at nine weeks; then she was expecting twins only to be told that one of them was severely brain damaged. The brain-damaged child was aborted at thirty weeks while six hours later the other twin, a boy, was born.[57] When trying for another IVF child and after three unsuccessful IVF cycles, she found an egg donor. The embryos were implanted in her womb, but her husband broke under the strain and asked for a divorce when she was eight weeks pregnant with twins. Since she couldn't imagine being a single mother with three children, she aborted the children she had desired so much. Her life is now in shambles with a failed marriage, depression, abortions, and apparently post-traumatic stress disorder.

As she states herself, part of the problem was her obsession about having children and being willing to sacrifice everything else to achieve this goal. But the reproductive technologies, I would add, simply acted as "enablers" to continue her fanatical quest for children. They did not offer her a real solution when she needed to go through an inner transformation. They simply postponed the crisis that destroyed her life in many ways. She recognizes them as being problematic but is not aware to what extent that is the case.

Couples may well experience their infertility as a strain on their marriage, but the added burden of having a donor child can make matters worse. One donor child (conceived through sperm insemination), now in her sixties, said: "I believe that . . . [my mother] carrying a child conceived by another man's sperm and raising that child caused [my father] a deep hurt."[58] In such a situ-

---

[57] *Dignitas Personae* interestingly points out this contradiction: "The decision to eliminate human lives, given that it was a human life that was desired in the first place, represents a contradiction that can often lead to suffering and feelings of guilt lasting for years" (DP 21).

[58] Marquardt, Glenn, and Clark, *My Daddy's Name Is Donor*, p. 41.

ation, the child will experience the pain of her parents, carrying a burden that should not be hers.

Hence *Donum Vitae* defends not just the dignity of the spouses but also emphasizes the needs of the child who can only fully flourish when surrounded by married, loving parents:

> The fidelity of the spouses in the unity of marriage involves reciprocal respect of their right to become a father and a mother only through each other. The child has the right to be conceived, carried in the womb, brought into the world and brought up within marriage: it is through the secure and recognized relationship to his own parents that the child can discover his own identity and achieve his own proper human development. The parents find in their child a confirmation and completion of their reciprocal self-giving: the child is the living image of their love, the permanent sign of their conjugal union, the living and indissoluble concrete expression of their paternity and maternity. (DV chap. 2, § 1)[59]

---

[59] Though the percentage of divorce is not much higher for the parents of donor-conceived children than for those born to their biological parents (27% vs. 25%), it is telling that those divorces happen late in the marriage while most other divorces happen early on. The marriage survived the strain of infertility, but not that of conceiving a child through the help of a donor. Also, there are more family transitions within donor child families. Compared to 22% among adopted children, 44% experienced family transitions (divorces, remarriages, new live-in partners, losing contact with one parent, etc. (Marquardt, Glenn, and Clark, *My Daddy's Name Is Donor*, p. 43). It makes perfect sense. De facto, the wife is carrying another man's child; though it was not conceived through an adulterous sexual act, the woman is still impregnated by another man's sperm. In contrast, the parents of adopted children are much less likely to get divorced (14% rather than the 25% or 27%). So, the issue seems to center on donor-conception striking at the very heart of the love between the man and the woman. Unfortunately, it

Science

You might find it challenging to navigate through this maze of options that science offers these days. So I encourage you to take the time to read the documents the Church has put together to explain the justice, truth, and rationality of the laws that exist for our greater good so that we may speak the language of love through our acts at all times. *Donum Vitae, Humanae Vitae, Evangelium Vitae,* and the relevant passages in the Catechism can be found on the Vatican website. These need to be read with an open mind and a sincere desire to discover the truth and do what is right. That will require some effort. We often falsely expect that we should be easily convinced by the arguments, when it really requires much thought and attention to understand them. Some truths that were obvious sixty years ago are no longer so, especially when our deepest wishes go against them. At the very least, I believe one should make an informed decision with the desire to do the right thing rather than being guided merely by one's great desire for a child. And even if we do not understand everything, let us trust the Church, our Mother, whom God has given us to protect us from an abyss of sin and misery.

Let me conclude this point on a personal note: My husband and I are tremendously grateful for the Church's guidance in our journey of infertility. The Church's positions always made sense to us. It was when encountering options on which the Church had not yet pronounced herself that we felt the full weight of making a responsible choice. The temptation then was either to be overly scrupulous or to be swept away by our desire for a child and fail to see the problems involved. The Church gave us the signposts for

---

took the suffering of many donor-conceived children to be able to show this statistically.

our journey, for which we are eternally grateful. We try to do the same for other infertile couples by showing the reasonability and wisdom of the Church's teachings.

The Church, by the way, has no problem with science as such. As *Donum Vitae* clearly states, it is not the artificiality of the procedure which constitutes the problem. A heart pacemaker is also artificial but poses no moral problems—on the contrary. But all scientific measures must be given a moral evaluation in reference to the dignity of the person.[60] A pacemaker does not negatively affect human dignity, but to be brought into existence outside of the context of the spousal act does.

The fact that IVF is widely used does not tell us anything about its ethical standing (slavery was widely accepted in the past, for example, but that does not justify it). But it is difficult to see this when pain, personal interest, cultural pressure, and money are involved.

LOVE VERSUS INSTRUMENTALIZATION

As *Donum Vitae* states so clearly, the dignity of the human person demands that every child be the fruit of his parents' spousal union.[61] He must be conceived as the fruit of his parents' love instead of being produced in a petri dish by technicians. It is hard to imagine a greater contrast than that between being conceived through a spousal embrace and in a lab. The fact that the parents desire that child and will treat it with great love afterward does not change the nature of their coming-into-being in a lab in a utilitarian manner. We have perhaps become too used to this method to be

---

[60] DV introduction, § 1.
[61] DV chap. 2, § 1.

shocked by its intrinsic contempt for human dignity. A hundred years ago, our ancestors would have been scandalized, not because they were puritanical, but because they would have recognized its instrumentalizing nature, to which we have become blind. They would have understood more easily that a child is not "made," that they should never be treated like a product, but that they have to be conceived in a context of love. They need human warmth and not a clinical coldness that chooses which children will be allowed to live and which are to die.

Only unconditional, gratuitous love is the proper response to the human person. It is the context in which they should come into being, the way they should be approached during their whole life, and should support them during suffering and death. God has given us life out of love as a gift, and that is the way we should transmit it as well.[62] Theoretically, people may have problems accepting that, but deep down everyone craves love and is hurt when treated as a means rather than an end. Some IVF-conceived adults suffer from the fact that their existence was "paid for," as if they were a commodity that can be bought. Donor-conceived Christine Whipp writes: "My existence owed almost nothing to the serendipitous nature of normal human reproduction, where babies are the natural progression of mutually fulfilling adult relationships, but rather represented a verbal contract, a financial transaction and a cold, clinical harnessing of medical technology."[63]

---

[62] As *Evangelium Vitae* says: "Thus the deepest element of God's commandment to protect human life is the requirement to show reverence and love for every person and the life of every person" (EV 41). And, "In giving life to man, God demands that he love, respect and promote life. The gift thus becomes a commandment, and the commandment is itself a gift" (EV 52).

[63] Marquardt, Glenn, and Clark, *My Daddy's Name Is Donor*, p. 23.

As *Donum Vitae* states about the difference between the two different kinds of conception:

> In reality, the origin of a human person is the result of an act of giving. The one conceived must be the fruit of his parents' love. He cannot be desired or conceived as the product of an intervention of medical or biological techniques; that would be equivalent to reducing him to an object of scientific technology. No one may subject the coming of a child into the world to conditions of technical efficiency which are to be evaluated according to standards of control and dominion. (DV chap. 2, § 4c)

Of course, those conceiving children naturally are also called to receive them like a gift in every respect; otherwise, they will inflict severe wounds on them. Many parents find that they cannot sound out the mystery of this new person who, despite their similarities, is still someone other and separate from themselves. They do not "own" them. Similarly, in every relationship, the love of another cannot be forced. We tend to feel this keenly when suffering from unrequited love.

But we need to rediscover this truth when it comes to the conception of a child. To force things means using the other for the satisfaction of one's own needs and desires. A utilitarian intention destroys love and undermines any relationship. IVF, which is intrinsically utilitarian, saps the parent-child relationship in its very beginning; however much the child is loved afterwards, their first moments happened outside the context of love. If I am already instrumentalized from the first moment of my existence, where will I find the certitude that I am loved for my own sake? And if I know that my siblings have been killed for being less perfect or simply put in limbo through freezing, there is a high chance I will spend the rest of my life trying to justify my existence by being either a perfectionist or rebelling, since the burden is too crushing.

Not only IVF but also artificial insemination poses an ethical problem since the sperm is collected in an act of masturbation. This separates sexuality from its proper context and meaning, which is to express itself in an act of love toward one's spouse that is open to life. Given the current culture, it may be difficult to understand that masturbation constitutes a grave sin. But sexuality reaches into the deepest core of our being—that is why it is such a powerful expression of the gift of self but also so destructive when used outside of the right context. If misused, it can create deep wounds in our psyche and soul. No sexual act is insignificant or morally neutral. Used outside of the context of love for which marriage sets the stage, even if "merely" for a medical intervention, it is profoundly out of place.[64]

Similarly, the sample for a sperm test which is necessary to

---

[64] Whether the use of sperm collected from a spousal act (in a pierced condom) which is medically treated and then re-inserted into the woman is ethically licit or not, has not been determined by the Church so far. Some moral theologians argue that this method does not interrupt the spousal act, but only assists it in its completion, while others come to the conclusion that it does constitute an interruption and is therefore morally illicit. The fundamental question is whether the IUI (Intrauterine Insemination) "assists" or "replaces" the conjugal act. If the semen is injected into the uterus via a catheter in a clinic setting and on top of this sperm "washing" takes place in between, it is doubtful that an adequate link to the conjugal act exists to qualify as assistance rather than replacement. Instead of facilitating the natural act, IUI seems distinct and a substitute for that loving embrace. It would seem to me that a technique far more likely to assist the conjugal act would be one that collected semen with a pierced condom and then injected the semen directly to the opening of the cervix immediately by the husband as a continuation of the act of conjugal union.

diagnose the causes of a couple's infertility should not be collected through masturbation, as most laboratories suggest. There are some alternatives: A pierced condom can be used to allow for the possibility of conception while permitting the sperm to be collected as the result of a spousal embrace (this means most of the time having to put one's foot down, since the laboratories prefer masturbation, where 100% of the semen is collected). Another approach is to have a doctor look at the sperm in the woman's vagina within an hour after intercourse. The doctor will be able to get a sperm count as well as establish the percentage of healthy versus unhealthy sperm.

The empirical data concerning artificial reproductive technologies, that is, the personal witnesses of donor-conceived children, its effects on marriage, the instrumentalization of the couples, the donors, and the children that I have presented so far, empirically confirms the natural law. Respect for the dignity of the human person must come first; when it doesn't, much suffering is the consequence. The technologies described attack that dignity in multiple ways, using the persons involved, and have led to innumerable deaths. But even if no extra babies were created in the process, even if no children were to die, it would still be unethical to bring forth children in that way.

The Intrinsic Dignity of the Human Person and Marriage

Is the Church saying that children conceived through IVF have less worth in God's eyes since they were brought into existence in a manner that is contrary to His laws? Of course not. Every human life has infinite value in the eyes of God: whether a child is born in or out of wedlock, is the result of a rape, or is the product of *in vitro* fertilization (not that they are equal!), this does not change the dignity of the child. It is precisely *because* of their infinite value that the Church defends so strongly their right to be surrounded by love at all times, from conception until birth and until natural death. *Donum Vitae* emphasizes that point, when it states: "The one conceived must be the fruit of his parents' love. He cannot be desired or conceived as the product of an intervention of medical or biological techniques; that would be equivalent to reducing him to an object of scientific technology" (DV chap. 2, § 4c).

The sacrament of marriage gives the ideal, loving context into which a child is born. If their parents are not married, are divorced, or are separated, the chance of being destabilized and experiencing a tremendous amount of emotional pain greatly increases. The sacramental union of their parents who love each other gives them a solid foundation on which they can build their identity. If their parents—though married—do not treat each other or them in a loving way then of course they are again in grave danger of being deeply hurt. Marriage is not a guarantee for love, but it sets the best conditions for its flowering. It is not a guarantee against abuse and violence since that still depends on the free choice of the spouses, who may decide not to be true to their vows.

Even if a child has a less-than-ideal starting point because they are conceived through IVF, or abortions have happened in the family, or their parents separate, one need not despair. God writes straight on crooked lines when we put our trust in Him. However difficult a situation may be, nothing is lost and God will never abandon us. If we give Him free reign, His grace can transform everything. There are consequences for all of our actions, and our suffering won't necessarily disappear, but some good will come out of it, even if we might only see this fully in the next life.

The child owes their existence to the individual creative act of

God, who brings into existence each human soul when the sperm fertilizes the egg; the parents are only procreators, but their role is a beautiful one, for out of their love another being comes into existence. God always creates in an act of love—human beings are less reliable, but have the duty to do the same. So what the Church really defends in its moral pronouncements is a law of life, as *Donum Vitae* underlines, that leads to fulfillment and happiness, even though it means embracing the Cross at times. However hard it may be to refrain from using IVF, the Church does not defend these laws in order to make our life harder but in order to protect us from destructive choices.

An Alternative and Promising Treatment

The Church encourages the treatment of infertility, helping the parents conceive children by their own means rather than having their offspring produced for them. Infertility treatment should assist the parents in conceiving children rather than replace the parents through technology. Most couples suffering from infertility would prefer that anyway—that is my guess—but just don't know there are options other than IVF.

As a starting point (if one isn't already using one), fertility awareness-based methods like the Billings method are a good to utilize because they pinpoint the woman's fertile period and thus allow for easier conception. But if this doesn't yield any results, then it makes sense to turn to the more sophisticated method of the Creighton Model FertilityCare System (CrMS) developed by Dr. Thomas Hilgers at the Pope Paul VI Institute in Omaha, Nebraska. It has a high success rate, with 76% of normally fertile couples who conscientiously apply it (based on the careful monitoring of the woman's cycle and the observation of her cervical mucus (length, consistency, color), conceiving within the *first month* of using it, which is a very high rate even for fertile couples. Of couples with infertility issues, 20%–40% conceive within the first six months of using CrMS.[65] Some of these couples had already tried IVF, but without any success.[66] Setting aside the ethical issues, such couples obviously did not need such an invasive method as IVF, since they were able to conceive by knowing exactly when the woman was ovulating.

Women who have endometriosis or other health issues which make conception difficult can benefit from Dr. Hilgers' NaProTechnology, which includes a very sophisticated surgical treatment. For example, 81.8% of women conceived who had suffered from anovulation (lack of ovulation), and 56.7% of women suffering from endometriosis achieved pregnancy, while only 21.2% with the same condition gave birth after using IVF.[67]

Fertility-awareness methods are wonderful alternatives to IVF that neither go against the dignity of the child nor of the parents, have a higher success rate, and carry less risks. First, for example, one learns how to use the Creighton method, then one's chart is sent to a doctor trained in the method who can give a partial diagnosis, deciding whether a laparoscopy is necessary to determine the presence of endometriosis or not. If there isn't too much of it, then it is immediately removed during the laparoscopy; otherwise, it will take another surgery.

Charting one's fertility can help give practitioners the

---

[65] Thomas W. Hilgers, *Creighton Model FertilityCare System: An Authentic Language of a Woman's Health and Fertility*, 5th ed. (Omaha, NE: Pope Paul VI Institute Press, 2001), p. 53.

[66] NaProTechnology has a much higher success rate than IVF as the statistics show. "Infertility," NaProTechnology, accessed January 10, 2021, https://naprotechnology.com/infertility/.

[67] "Infertility."

detailed information they need to make other diagnoses as well, such as polycystic ovarian syndrome, low progesterone, tumors on the pituitary gland that impact fertility, uterine septum, MTHFR gene mutation, and other disorders.

ADDRESSING THE PAIN OF INFERTILITY: MAKING A LOVING CHOICE

One of the strongest reasons for turning to IVF is the suffering of infertile couples who are willing to undergo many difficulties in order to carry that much-desired baby in their arms. Only a child, it seems to them, would free them from this crushing pain. Merely telling them the risks they might encounter is often not enough to help them change their mind. Giving them a promising alternative is one way, though no method can guarantee success. Letting them hear the voices of children who have suffered from ART gives them a much-needed perspective on these procedures. If they realized that they might well inflict great suffering on them, worse than their own pain, they would be more willing to give up attempting IVF. For their hurt, while great, does not strike at the heart of love like the instrumentalization of another through IVF. They are not experiencing a rejection, though they have to mourn their loss. Their pain and that of children born through IVF or surrogacy is therefore not comparable; it is of a different kind. Infertility is a human tragedy, while IVF goes against love and the child will have to bear the consequences of this.

Couples who try to escape the pain of infertility are simply shifting their suffering to their children. As the donor-conceived Lynne Burns states: "Infertility can mean mourning the loss of someone who has never existed. However, choosing donor conception to overcome infertility can mean transferring the loss so that it is now the child who grieves, in this case for someone they have also never met, the missing biological parent."[68] This is the couples' choice: their suffering or that of their potential offspring (for IVF-conceived persons, whether they are donor-conceived or not, can suffer from the mode of their coming-into-being, as I've shown).

If true parental feeling can be stirred in their heart, their choice will be selfless. For love always wants the good of the other; otherwise, it is egotistical and instrumentalizes the other which, according to St. John Paul II, is the opposite of love, even more than hatred. Like that mother in King Solomon's times who preferred to lose her child rather than see him killed, the infertile couple will choose what is best for their potential child. The infertile couple may not have the gratification of having a child. Yet their choice is similar—it is that between their pain or another's. They therefore act as real parents who want the best for their children. They become, in a certain sense, spiritual parents, for they make a choice that all parents with children of their own are called to make.

As St. Mother Teresa pointed out, the meaning of love is to give until it hurts. In this world, the Cross is part of love. If one tries to flee it, one still won't be able to escape pain in the long run while losing what is most important, namely love. And without love, suffering becomes unbearable.

---

[68] Burns, "Laura Burns 'Donor Conceived' Perspective."

Chapter 6

HOW TO DEAL WITH INFERTILITY

The question still remains of how to deal with the pain of infertility on an everyday basis. Those who make the heroic choice of not doing IVF (and those for whom IVF hasn't worked) might have to face a life without children or less children than they would like. Even if hopefully only temporary, this painful period should not simply be lost time that they try to forget as quickly as possible.

For those who are given reason to believe they should be able to have children, but find themselves childless, confidence and distress alternate until menopause ends all remaining hope. Others learn early on that they are sterile, that they will never have any biological children, which comes as a tremendous shock. They won't have any false expectations, but will be stopped in their tracks and have to face their childlessness all at once, which might be even harder.

The Importance of Surrender

As I've emphasized, it is important that we permit ourselves to mourn. Humanly speaking, it may seem impossible to accept the emptiness that infertility leaves. The pain easily becomes obsessive and is one of the features of affliction, according to Simone Weil.[1] Certain sufferings leave permanent scars; we will never be the same again. Some women have told me that this new sad self is not who they are, that they are really cheerful and outgoing, but that this pain has worn them down. It is helpful to understand that this is what happens when tragedy strikes: we are no longer the same afterwards. Breaking points may differ; some may come out of a similar situation fairly whole. But everyone has a breaking point—the question is when and whether he is ever pushed to the point of having to experience it or not.

These seemingly life-destroying wounds—these deep desires that we have had to abandon—can paradoxically become paths of life, if they are accepted. But it is precisely this acceptance that often seems downright impossible. Though—appearances notwithstanding—it is possible, it does take time. Surrendering our will to God's (who for whatever reason is not lifting this suffering from us, even if He didn't send it) can take a long time. We may say "yes" on one level, thinking we are done, but not on others that we still need to work through. Surrendering isn't like jumping through hoops. It means accepting a crushing cross against which our nature rebels. We need to be patient with ourselves; our nature takes time to be leavened through. But the more we resist, the harder it is going to be.

One thing is certain, namely that we cannot cut corners.

---

[1] Simone Weil, *Œuvres complètes*, bk. 6, vol. 1: *Cahiers (1933–Septembre 1941)*, ed. Alyette Degrâces et al. (Paris: Gallimard, 1944), p. 142.

By trying to do so we are simply avoiding the mourning process which we still need to go through. Avoidance or shortening the process won't help. Only surrender will give relief.

ACCEPTING THE PRESENT MOMENT

Thinking of the years stretching ahead without children (or less than one would like) may seem impossible to accept. But I am not asked to agree now to what the future may yield, but only to the present moment. For now, just this second, I am asked to consent to my infertility—and this will probably seem more doable. I don't know how I will feel about infertility once menopause comes along, or old age for that matter. Perhaps I will experience things differently then, even if that seems highly unlikely now. New graces, inner growth, other events in my life might shift things for me in unpredictable ways.

Bad memories of the past can make us apprehensive about the future. But the first is over, while the other isn't here yet. Only the present is given to me. It's in the present that I encounter God, that I live life fully, that I love, and that I gain eternal life. I don't know what tomorrow will bring or if I will have a tomorrow. Each day has enough trouble of its own. Only for now do I need to embrace this cross—not for years to come.

There will be times of trial where we think we cannot stand it any longer; and then there will be moments of greater serenity. As time goes on, the periods of serenity will probably become longer, though this does not mean that the pain will ever completely disappear.[2] Just like parents who lose a child will never stop feeling

---

[2] For some, the pain will seem to get worse rather than better. Their hearts are broken and nothing, it seems, can mend them. I can only encourage those who go through such heartbreak to seek help. Their suffering is terrible—there is

their loss yet eventually reach some peace, so this pain will eventually be borne with greater calm in one's heart.

Attending a Retreat

I never thought I'd be able to accept having no or less than two or three children. After the birth of our daughter, I immediately wanted to become pregnant again, and each time I'd drive past the hospital where I'd given birth, I felt a pang, hoping I'd be there again soon. However, our hopes were dashed. After a miscarriage which—though devastating—gave us hope that more children were to come, nothing happened. We didn't give up for a long time, though my biological clock told us we ought to. What helped me the most was attending a Rachel's Vineyard retreat.

Though they are set up for people who have suffered from abortion(s), I was allowed to attend. In this instance, most of the other attendees were there for reasons other than past abortions, mostly in order to get a certificate that would allow them to become assistants at future retreats; they therefore simply mourned their personal losses whatever those were. It was a cathartic experience. I wept for three days, but this mourning process lightened my heart as nothing had done before. I still go through times of sadness, even of weeping, but my heart is free of that crushing pain that I experienced without any break for many years.

---

no doubt about it—and their past, character, and many factors all contribute to this feeling. But this does not mean that there is no way of improving it, even if it they do not have the resources in themselves to do so. It is precisely in these cases that a good therapist is of the essence—and sometimes it takes some research to find the right one. From a spiritual perspective, it is a good idea to pray to Our Lady, whose heart was broken as well and who went through agonies of pain.

Grief and Inner Joy: Chiara Corbella

If we feel crushed by the experience of infertility and have the impression that we must be therefore responding inadequately to it, this does not mean that we are doing anything wrong. Sometimes, we are under the false impression that being abandoned to God's will means that in Herculean fashion we will sail through these trials, be a witness to the world through our inner and outer strength, and that we somehow won't experience so much pain. But being nailed to the Cross means experiencing great anguish. Even Christ did—and He is the Son of God. The only thing we can do is depend on Him, allow Him into our pain, and ask Him to help. This alone will give inner peace.

Chiara Corbella is a perfect example of this. In 2012, she died from cancer at the age of twenty-eight in order to save her unborn child whom she didn't want to hurt through aggressive chemotherapy. Her story exemplifies how a long and painful journey can lead to great inner peace and joy by advancing just little steps at a time (*piccolo passi*), as she and her husband liked to say.

This ultimate sacrifice had been prepared by others: half an hour after their births, the Corbella's first two children had died from serious, unrelated handicaps. Each time Chiara and her husband Enrico were expecting to feel crushed by their fate, but instead they were carried by an inner joy that could not be explained, humanly speaking. God had entrusted these children to them for a brief period, during which they gave them all their love and had them baptized.

While Chiara lay dying fourteen months after the birth of her third child, who was in good health, her husband asked her if the Cross was *dolce* (sweet), as Jesus had promised. She answered that it was *molto dolce*. She had received a particular grace, illuminating the mystery of the Cross. In the darkest abyss of suffering, I can find Love who holds me in His arms, fulfills me, and consoles me.

However, to embrace the Cross isn't necessarily followed by interior joy. Everyone has their own individual vocation. Those who are going through depression, who have been deeply wounded or who, because of their past or disposition, feel like they are carrying the weight of the world, might not experience any joy. Some saints have even spent most of their existence in a dark night of the soul: St. Teresa of Calcutta during fifty years and St. Thérèse of Lisieux during the last years of her short life. In these cases, God's presence is so strong and intense that He overwhelms and blinds the soul, giving her the false impression that He is absent. However, this does not prevent people undergoing a dark night from radiating peace and even joy. For God is present in them and He manifests Himself through their whole being, though they may not experience Him while those around them can.

God's Thirst for Us: Mother Teresa

It was on a train going to Darjeeling that Mother Teresa received her vocation to serve the poorest of the poor. At the same time, she understood that God is thirsting for us, for our love. As Joseph Langford showed so well in his book *Mother Teresa's Secret Fire*, at the heart of her spirituality is God's desire to come into our "inner Calcuttas."[3] For poverty does not just mean lacking material goods, though that too should be remedied, but at its worst it is interior. We all carry in us the wounds of sin and suffering, these inner Calcuttas which we hide from ourselves and the world

---

[3] Joseph Langford, *Mother Teresa's Secret Fire: The Encounter that Changed Her Life and How It Can Transform Your Own* (Huntington, IN: Our Sunday Visitor, 2008).

because they seem too ugly, too dark, too painful. Yet God wants to enter precisely into these spaces where no one else can bring consolation and healing. He wants to unite Himself with us, *here and now*, in our misery.

So I shouldn't wait to be perfect (which is impossible in this life anyway) before letting God enter and offering Him a place in my suffering, for He wants nothing more than to unite Himself to me right here. If I allow Him in, I will never be alone again in my suffering—He went through it Himself on the Cross in order to be with us when we would be on ours. And my intense desire for children is only a pale reflection of His thirst for my love. I participate through my longing in Christ's suffering during His agony, when He cried out "I thirst," which was the ultimate expression of His love.

Choosing One's Counselors Well

For some, as already mentioned, the pain may become obsessive and turn into a depression; then it might be a good idea to get some counseling, preferably from a Christian therapist who will take into account the spiritual dimension of the issue. Or it could be beneficial to find a good priest and talk to him. In either case, I need not wait until experiencing full-blown depression before seeking help. But I need to choose prudently with whom I talk. This can be hard, for when suffering intensely, I can find it difficult to hold back in my desperate attempt to find someone who will give me the love and empathy that bring relief. But if I don't, then I risk having my pain overflow in the presence of random people who might not have any psychological finesse and will unintentionally hurt me.

I have found that talking to other women who are undergoing

the same trial can be very helpful. To see that one is not alone, that others struggle with the same things (and have probably been hurt by the same kind of comments), and to witness how they are coping can be encouraging.

Making Use of This Time

Not having children often means having more time on one's hands. It makes sense to take advantage of this period in the desert when God lets you depend on Him alone: turn this into a spiritual journey rather than letting it simply be a human disaster. This is a time of growing closer to Him, of accepting His holy will, however painful it is. Whether God will eventually bless you with children or not, you will have grown through this experience.

So use this time well: get involved in projects you may never be able to do again. Serving the Church and other people lovingly is a wonderful thing.[4] Our suffering can potentially make us more empathetic to the suffering of others and therefore help us to be open to assisting them. But there is a right time for everything. If I am exhausted or depressed, then it might be better to treat myself with tender loving care and give myself a break rather than trying to "save the world."

---

[4] "Spouses who still suffer from infertility after exhausting legitimate medical procedures should unite themselves with the Lord's Cross, the source of all spiritual fecundity. They can give expression to their generosity by adopting abandoned children or performing demanding services for others." CCC 2379.

TRUSTING GOD

We tend to be afraid that uniting ourselves to Christ, or abandoning ourselves to God's will, might make matters worse; perhaps He will ask for something that is too hard; perhaps He will ask more, simply because we are more ready to do so. Sometimes the lives of saints seem filled with atrocious sufferings while their inner joy, which is the fruit of their union with God and gives more happiness than anything else, remains hidden to us. If I only see the negative side, then my understanding of God is skewed, and I will perceive Him as a sadistic tyrant who begrudges us our happiness. But nothing could be further from the truth.

God wants our happiness. He did not create infertility—it is a sickness and hence a consequence of original sin. In the beginning, He gave Adam and Eve the task to populate the earth (Gen 1:28). Yes, He is master over life and death, and He can determine even miraculously to give a sterile couple the blessing of a child. But most of the time He bows down humbly to the human condition in its brokenness. Just as He wants children to be conceived by the loving self-gift of spouses and born into a loving family but also allows children to be conceived in cases of adultery and rape, so He permits people's bodily brokenness to affect their capacity to be procreators. So let us not turn away from Him, thinking that He simply does not wish us to be parents. Our sorrow will be the greater, our wounds will fester, and deep unhappiness will be the result while joyful peace is still possible if we accept that cross.

Certain pains never disappear; they break one's heart and closure seems impossible. They age with us as we grow older. This kind of suffering brands us for life; it breaks, shapes, molds us.

We have two paths in front of us: that of life and that of death, as God says in Deuteronomy (30:15). The choice is between giving and taking, receiving and grasping, accepting life as a gift or seeing it as something to which one is entitled. In the first case, children are received as a gift, in the second they are not. Allowing ourselves to be vulnerable and perhaps not receiving the gift of children means speaking the language of love, even if heartbreaking. "Producing" a child at all costs, no matter what the consequences, is ultimately a path of death, since need and not love is its source.

Yes, children are a great good; they often bring great happiness, and life without them may seem dreary and empty. But even they, being finite, cannot fulfill the infinite longing of the human heart. Only God can do so, and only He can console us for our losses, and mend our broken hearts. Then we will realize that Golgotha initiates the new Eden: the Cross becomes the new Tree of Life.

The Mystery of Suffering

Suffering in all of its forms remains a mystery. Yes, there are explanations for it, such as original sin. But this does not yet answer the anguished question as to why this misfortune is happening to me or to someone dear to me. God does not explain to Job the reason for his suffering. But He does give an answer—the only answer which can satisfy the heart, which is God Himself. For, as the French philosopher and mystic Simone Weil says, though "affliction renders God absent during a certain time, more absent than the dead, more absent than the light in a completely dark dungeon," the soul will ultimately hear "silence itself as something infinitely fuller of significance than any answer, as the word itself of God. The soul knows then that the absence of God here below is the same as the secret presence here below of that God that is in heaven."[5]

---

[5]   Simone Weil, *Intuitions pré-chretiennes* (Paris: Fayard, 1985), p. 168.

Or as John Paul II writes in *Salvifici Doloris*:

> For Christ does not answer directly and he does not answer in the abstract this human questioning about the meaning of suffering. Man hears Christ's saving answer as he himself gradually becomes a sharer in the sufferings of Christ. The answer which comes through this sharing, by way of the interior encounter with the Master, is in itself *something more than the mere abstract answer* to the question about the meaning of suffering. For it is above all a call. It is a vocation. Christ does not explain in the abstract the reasons for suffering, but before all else he says: "Follow me!" Come! (SD 26)

It is hard to follow that call when it includes a crushing cross that doesn't seem to be going away. At the same time, the choice of rebellion or lingering resentment is not a solution since it doesn't resolve anything and only causes more suffering. The Cross, I'd be tempted to say, is part of the fabric of our lives since the Fall. No one, not even the most outspoken atheist, can avoid suffering. Even on a natural level, it needs to be accepted (when it cannot be changed) if one wants to lead a fulfilling and meaningful life. Love itself requires self-sacrifice, going against one's egoism and pride, and this is painful. In contrast, life without love becomes hell on earth.

"Do not be afraid," as John Paul II exclaimed at the beginning of his pontificate. We are afraid of crosses, of the deaths we experience through them. But by accepting them, God will bless us a hundredfold and we will bear fruit for the Church and the world—perhaps in ways we may never know. Christ carries His wounds for eternity and so will we, if we embrace them. Our wounds will be part of our glory, shining forth, reflecting God in a particular way.

Though we may never have biological children, we will have spiritual children in heaven and we might only get to know many of them in the next life. This may seem a meager consolation for those brokenhearted by their childlessness who want to have a baby in their arms now instead of being dished out some far-off promise. We have the tendency to view spiritual filiation as a distant relationship with little gratification for one's motherly or paternal feelings. However, we know that what we were denied or gave up in this life will be given to us superabundantly. Mother- and fatherhood on earth are but a pale reflection of what we will experience in eternity. Psalm 113 announces that barren women will have many children. God does not make false promises. What was already good on earth will attain its fulfillment in heaven. We can therefore imagine ourselves in heaven surrounded by children, carrying babies in our arms whom we can hug and kiss.

Though our cross is often hidden to the world since it is easily assumed that we are contracepting, our infertility—if we live it well—will contribute to the construction of a civilization of love. Our heroic choice not to use IVF, the acceptance of our cross as part of the plan of God for our lives is a spiritual reality that has vast effects. By uniting ourselves to Christ we are "carrying out an irreplaceable service" in view of the salvation of our brothers and sisters, as John Paul II states in *Salvifici Doloris*. For we are "clear[ing] the way for the grace which transforms human souls. Suffering, more than anything else, makes present in the history of humanity the powers of the Redemption" (SD 27).

Furthermore, our choices, our attitudes, and our values will radiate forth. We will be showing to the world that children are not commodities, that they are gifts whether they are handicapped, wanted, smart, handsome, loved, or not. No one has a "right" to a child. Children are a precious blessing, and it is a great suffering not to have any or less than we would wish. By accepting this cross out of God's hand, we are becoming true children of God, for we are living in receptivity to God's will instead of making ourselves masters over life and death. God will reward us in manifold and unexpected ways—but the full extent of this will only become clear in eternity, for in the meantime we continue to see everything through a glass darkly.

A PERSONAL POSTSCRIPT

Whathen I wrote the first, brief version of this book in 2006, we did not know what the future would hold. Some doctors gave us hope. Others didn't. Like many infertile couples, we were going through many ups and downs, wondering whether a baby might just be around the corner or whether we would remain childless for the rest of our lives. When we learned at the end of January 2009 that we were expecting, we were filled with overwhelming gratitude. We had some worrying moments during the pregnancy, but after nine years of marriage, on September 29, 2009, on the feast day of the archangels, our little Thérèse Marie was born—healthy, lean, and long, with big, thoughtful eyes.

Hundreds of people all over the world had prayed for us. Many helped us to make this miracle baby possible. God and man worked together to bring this new person into the world. I'd like to share some parts of this grace-filled story. But before I do, I want to make a few points that will shed light on our journey and might be helpful to others.

Infertility is a complex condition. Frequently, both spouses have issues, and the roots of these problems are varied. This makes a complete diagnosis difficult. Over the years, we therefore tried to address the problem from three angles—namely from the physical, psychological, and spiritual perspectives—hoping we would eventually reach the tipping point. We needed to get a grasp of the different physical problems involved in our infertility and sought the advice of a variety of doctors going at it with their own methods, be they standard or off-the-beaten-path. Discernment was not easy, but we tried to be open to what seemed promising and sensible even if unusual and we tried to avoid the quacks as well as overly invasive treatments. To some extent, we had to go by trial and error; only a successful pregnancy would tell us if we'd gotten things right.

While the physical side of infertility is complex enough, the psychological one isn't any easier. We are all wounded by original sin, by events in our life, and we carry our family's history with its specific burdens. No one is completely whole. And the experience of long-lasting infertility can add new wounds or make old ones break out again. All of this can further impede our fertility. If infertility is experienced as paralyzing, as a roadblock beyond which no full life or happiness seems possible, then we may do well to consider getting some help. This can be as simple as getting some good books or going to a counselor a few times or as much as getting full therapy.[1] It is normal to suffer and to suffer greatly from infertility; it would be wrong to think that this is a sign of psychological sickness. But when that pain becomes incapacitating, when it starts to fester, it makes sense to seek some assistance.[2]

---

[1] I highly recommend Simone Pacot's *Evangelizing the Depths: A Pathway to Inner Unity*, trans. Roger W. T. Wilkinson (Eugene, OR: Cascade Books, 2019). She shows that we are wounded by sins against love, be it by our parents, siblings, spouses, friends, or by our own sins and disordered relationships. Even as baptized and practicing Christians, we are often unaware of these profound hurts and compensate for them in wrong ways, which can lead to psychological illnesses. The key is to let Christ enter these places so that He can heal us from the very depths of our being.

[2] This does not contradict my earlier point that one should abstain from

As my husband and I came to see, the spiritual aspect of the question was not to be underestimated either. Yes, we knew that God allowed us to carry this cross for our salvation and that of the world. Yes, we wanted, in principle, to grow on this journey (which doesn't mean that we always did or dealt with it rightly). We desired to give a full-hearted "yes" to God in this situation, but that proved to be very difficult. I came to see that saying "yes" to our infertility for this day, for this hour, or just for this moment was much easier than thinking of it in terms of a lifetime; taking it one step at a time, minute by minute was feasible with the grace of God, though still painful. And yes, we knew that prayer was very important. We prayed, went on pilgrimages, asked people to pray for us, offered up our pain, knowing that God would hear our prayers in some form though we were not sure, of course, that He would give us a baby.

Then we came to see the importance of intergenerational healing, as well as the power of prayers of deliverance. The idea here is that we carry not only the wounds from our immediate time and environment, but that these can be passed on from across

---

insinuating that the couple's infertility is caused by psychological problems and that all they need to do is get their act together. Apart from lacking the empathy of love (which alone helps one bear this cross) and often drawing on primitive categories of pop psychology, it leaves the couple in their suffering with a dose of guilt added to the mixture. Also, it claims a kind of omniscience which only God has, as if one could know with certitude the psychological reasons for infertility in an individual case; this is impossible because of the complexity of the problem and the mysterious nature of every individual. Since infertility can be, as already mentioned, a very complex issue, who is to say that psychological reasons are the exclusive or main roots of the problem? In any case, suggestions as to possible causes or therapies should only be raised in the context of love, with much tact and only if one senses that they are welcome.

generations.[3] Those who have taken up this idea have found that through the sacraments, especially Masses offered for the deceased and for our own healing, as well as through prayers for this intention, these wounds can be healed.

Sin and hurt tend to come in vicious cycles: people who have been sexually abused as children are more likely to do so to others, as we know from studies today; but even if they don't, they will carry deep wounds throughout their lives and will probably pass those on in some shape or form (for example, they might be depressed, particularly anxious, or controlling, all of which will have an impact on their surroundings). Or children whose parents have been divorced tend to be more fearful of commitments and more likely to get divorced themselves. They carry to different degrees the scars of their parents' decisions and hurts, and will probably pass these wounds on to their children down the line (and theirs to their own). People deal with suffering differently; some are more affected than others, and some wounds are more hidden while others are glaring and express themselves in neurotic forms. While psychology has its part to play, we are in need of Christ to bring these cycles to a halt.

Another aspect is our ancestors' need for prayer. They sinned just as we sin, suffered, and may have dealt badly with their trials; thus, they might still be in purgatory. Just as we carry each other's burdens in this life (a spouse, child, sibling, parent, or friend, for example, will suffer from the other's outbursts of anger,

---

[3] *Nota bene*: it is a question of *wounds* being transmitted, not of *sin*! Sins committed by me are my own and I carry the guilt for committing them. Though I cannot transfer my sins to others, unfortunately the consequences of my sins are also felt by others: the spouse I abandon, the child I abuse, the people whose money I stole or whose reputation I ruined will suffer from my acts for a long time.

impatience, or laziness), so we continue to do so with those who have already entered eternal life. We are all members of Christ's Mystical Body and share in each other's travails. Through our prayers and also our sufferings we can help each other; as St. Paul famously said: "Now I rejoice in my sufferings for your sake, and in my flesh I complete what is lacking in Christ's afflictions for the sake of his body, that is, the Church" (Col 1:24). Though Christ's redemptive suffering was complete, the application of its merits is not. By uniting our suffering to His we can help the outpouring of graces on others. Some deceased members of our family who did not sufficiently repent of their sins and did not give their sufferings over completely to Christ may therefore still be in dire need of prayer. Without this, we may well share their sufferings without knowing it; this might express itself in illnesses of all kinds. After we had gone through some intergenerational healing, my hormones (which had been skewed after a laparoscopy) went back to normal immediately. It was very striking.

Without Christ, our freedom is limited, and however much we try, we cannot help but be part of the domino effect of sin. Yes, we may lessen its impact over time to some extent through willpower, but we cannot gain complete freedom. This would imply that we can heal by ourselves the depths of our hearts. Instead, we need to acknowledge our weakness; this is fundamental to the spiritual life. Christ came to heal the sick, not those who think they are whole; hence we have to recognize that we are in need of help in the first place. Through the power of His redemptive sacrifice on Calvary, which is repeated at Mass, we are freed from the spiritual death of sin. We and our family members, both the living and the dead, are in need of this healing which is offered to us through the sacraments of the Church. In seeking it, we might well experience healing in other domains as well—physical and psychological.[4]

Already one's own sins can make one physically sick. I know a woman who had an abortion when she was young and who later suffered greatly from it, deeply regretting her choice. She was drawn to the Catholic Church because of the Sacrament of Confession, for she felt that only through this sacrament would she be freed of her guilt. In the meantime, she had married but was unable to have children, though the doctors couldn't find any medical reason for her infertility. Once she became a Catholic and went to confession, she conceived—something she attributed directly to the reception of the sacrament.

Another powerful tool for healing is the deliverance prayer. A priest said this prayer over us in January 2009, and very shortly thereafter we conceived. I could sense the authority the priest had through his office and felt how strong this prayer was. This prayer for deliverance is not an exorcism, thus any priest can say it. This deliverance prayer frees us from all curses, spells, and evil wishes that people may have directed against us. At first, I had a hard time understanding this, for I thought that Christ protected us through the Sacrament of Baptism and the many graces of the Church that we receive in the other sacraments. But just as others can hurt us through their words and acts, even to the point of murdering us, so they can hurt us spiritually (though they can never make us sin

---

[4] Sr. Briege McKenna's powerful healing ministry is based on these principles as well "St. Clare Sisters Retreat Ministry," Sr. Briege McKenna, O.S.C., accessed October 26, 2020, http://www.sisterbriege.com/srbriege.htm. I have found Fr. John H. Hampsch's approach helpful, which he presents in *Healing Your Family Tree*, 2nd ed. (Goleta, CA: Queenship, 1989). Kenneth McAll's book, *Healing the Family Tree* (London: Sheldon Press, 1982), is also interesting, for he presents intergenerational healing from a Protestant perspective.

against our will). Yes, we are protected and nothing happens to us without God's knowledge—He has counted every hair on our heads.[5] But He also lets us be part of this world with its trials and dangers. Since He takes our freedom very seriously, He allows us and others to use this freedom badly and against each other. We can be persecuted in different ways, including spiritually. Hence a deliverance prayer can be advisable in certain circumstances.

Because of my husband's pro-life work, for many years he was standing on the frontlines. All of us who try to follow God's will are there in some form or another and are thus potential targets. It is therefore not surprising that those who fight for life would be affected in their procreative capacity. God allows this to happen for our good and that of the world. My husband and I had the strong sense that we were meant to carry this suffering in reparation for the millions of sins against life in our day and age. At the same time, people all over the world and especially in the pro-life movement were praying for us, and we are immensely grateful to them. All of these prayers, the sacrifices made, the Blessed Mother, and the saints worked together to bring about the coming-into-existence of our little Thérèse.

In early January 2009, while a friend of mine was at daily Mass, she heard an inner voice telling her strongly during consecration that she should pray for me to conceive. She was very surprised since this kind of thing had never happened to her before. Did God need this further prayer on top of all the thousands which

---

[5] Therefore, we should not be fearful. It would be wrong to believe that psychological or spiritual wounds necessarily affect one's fertility. Many women become pregnant without wanting to even if they have had a number of abortions and even when they suffer from severe psychological illnesses. The point here is that these wounds *could* have a negative effect on fertility and that infertile couples therefore might want to seek healing in those areas.

had gone up to heaven already to give us a child? God didn't need it, but He desired it so that even more people would be spiritual mothers and father to our miracle child.

Though I always had a particular devotion to St Thérèse of Lisieux, I had not originally intended to give a child of ours this name. But my husband and I had a strong sense that she was supposed to be called Thérèse for the following reasons: In the summer of 2008, some nuns from India came up to my mother after Mass (this happened in Germany where my parents live). They expressed how sorry they were that I was still childless after so many years of marriage and wanted me to have a relic of St. Mother Teresa of Calcutta's sari, which had already helped many infertile couples, promising that they would pray for me every day. Though I had always admired St. Mother Teresa, she was not a saint to whom I felt a particular affinity. There were others toward whom I was more drawn to pray. Yet I did, though not as regularly as I should have. Interestingly, I had chosen her as my patron saint for the year of 2008, or rather she had chosen me (at the beginning of every year, I go to a website with a list of saints; I scroll up and down the screen with eyes closed, and thus let the saint choose me). For 2009, it was the newly beatified Martins, the parents of St Thérèse of Lisieux, who became my annual patron saints. But the Thérèsian theme didn't stop there, for our daughter's due date turned out to be October 1st, feast day of the Little Flower (which is significant, even though she came two days early, on the feast day of the archangels). As a middle name, we chose the name "Marie" in honor of Our Lady.

During my pregnancy, I came across Joseph Langford's wonderful book called *Mother Teresa's Secret Fire*, which opened up the spirituality of this saint in a new way. Though I had greatly appreciated Brian Kolodiejchuk's *Mother Teresa: Come Be My*

Light, Langford's book was life-changing, and I wished it had already appeared during our long years of infertility. Langford was one of the co-founders of the priestly branch of Mother Teresa's order and had a deep insight into her inner life. As a seminarian he had come across Malcolm Muggeridge's *Something Beautiful for God* and was deeply struck by Mother Teresa's photo and thoughts.

Mother Teresa had always been very discreet about the precise nature of her calling on the train to Darjeeling in 1946, but from the beginning Langford thought that there must be a connection between her mystical experience and the sign "I Thirst," which hangs next to the crucifix in every chapel of her order. He asked her many times about this, and she only slowly opened up to him. It was partially due to his encouragement, that she wrote her famous Varanasi letter toward the end of her life in 1993 where she speaks about Christ's thirst for our love. But she also told Langford that he should one day write about the connection between those two elements in her spirituality. Christ thirsts for us, which means He also thirsts for us to share our wounds, our sins, and weaknesses with Him. Deep down we tend to think that we are not loveable, that we first have to become perfect before God will love us. But God is eager to be allowed into our inner Calcuttas. For the worst sufferings, the worst Calcuttas, are not so much physical ones, though they are bad enough, but the sufferings stemming from sin—be it our own or that of others which victimizes us. When Mother Teresa said that we should bring Christ to our own Calcuttas, she therefore not only meant that we should care for the poor around us wherever we live, but also that we should let God into our own inner misery. No one but Christ can enter this place of pain and darkness, no one else can bring consolation and healing into this abyss. Yet we often lock Him out.

I read Langford's book during a time of crisis while I was pregnant. Not only was it tremendously helpful in a very difficult and painful situation, but I found that it was the best preparation for motherhood. For I was freed from many inner burdens which I had been carrying around and which couldn't but have affected my child as well. Hence Mother Teresa not only interceded for us to conceive a child but also helped me become a better mother.

I would love for our story to be a message of hope for those in the same predicament. Hearing about the happy ending of those whose situation seemed almost desperate can be encouraging to some, but it can also have the opposite effect on others; for the fact that some couples conceived late and against all odds obviously does not mean that one will do so oneself. I belonged more to the second group during our years of infertility. The reason for this was in part because these kinds of stories were sometimes told in a way forbidding me to mourn. The implication was, "You shouldn't be sad, for others who have been infertile longer than you and therefore have more right to complain still conceived." Or: "Don't let your pain get too close to me; let me tell you this story with a happy ending. If this doesn't give you hope, then the fault is yours." Let me add, however, that many people were sympathetic to our lot. Their tears of joy when we were finally able to announce that we were expecting were very touching.

Another reason for finding these stories painful rather than encouraging can be due to much inner pain, making it difficult to trust in God's love. Why should He give me children, one might feel deep down, when He has already allowed me to suffer so much in my life? Yet these moments—once we realize what is going on—can become the opportunity to face one's lack of trust in God, humbly acknowledge it, and ask God to come into one's inner darkness. One cannot heal this lack of confidence and this pain oneself. As the father of the sick son says to Jesus in the Gospels, we need to say "help my unbelief" (Mark 9:24). The greatest human disaster can become the opportunity for the greatest divine victory if we only let God act through this. If we won't, then our suffering will only get worse, for it will fester. It is very painful to let the divine doctor touch our wounds, just like it is painful to have a dentist treat an infected tooth. But the divine physician's touch is lighter and more efficient than any human one could be, yet we allow the latter to treat us for fear of greater pain, but often not the first.

God is with us in our suffering; we are never alone. He has heard our cries; He will not forget us. Let us all pray for an end to the sins against life. Let us encourage doctors to find real solutions to the modern phenomenon of increased infertility by healing couples rather than producing children in an anti-human way through IVF. Let us offer our pain in reparation for the terrible injustice of abortion and the tremendous pain these little ones have to go through, ripped apart by vacuum suction, their little bodies poisoned or chemically burned to death. Is there any feeling of rejection that can compare to theirs, when their mother, the person, upon whom they depend completely, decides they should die?[6] If we unite our pain to theirs, they will become

---

[6] Let me add, however, on a note of consolation for those women who have had abortions, that their children have forgiven them and are now with God in heaven. Even if their mothers rejected them at a certain moment, God never did and was with them in their greatest anguish.

Mothers are often under tremendous pressure to abort; they frequently say later that they felt they had "no choice," since it was their husbands, boy-friends, families, or difficult economic conditions which made them decide to have an abortion (hence manifesting the lie of the pro-choice slogan which is really a "no-choice" mentality of coercion and despair).

our spiritual children in heaven. They will greet us, when we get there, and our reward will be great.

September 8, 2021

*Some Essays on Connected Issues** *

HAVING "ONLY" ONE:
RAISING AN ONLY CHILD

We are living the dream—at least the dream according to the secular mind. We only have one child. Not by choice, mind you. We would love to have more and didn't expect to end up with just one. For a while it even looked like we would have none. This child was greatly desired, prayed for, and many tears were shed over the nine long years of marriage it took before God gave us this great gift. We were blessed. Some have none, while others have so many that they are struggling to manage. So why complain? And why speak of "only" one? Is it really that bad?

It is not, but it takes some mourning and adjusting. When interacting with one's secular friends, they can have a hard time understanding why the pain is so great not to have more (except if they've suffered from infertility themselves—then they *know*). It can be challenging to explain why this is so difficult. Or people assume that this is your choice, and you didn't want any more. Since the modern ideal is between one to two children, some people think that a sibling is a good idea (so do I, though I'd put that in the plural); so they'll make some helpful suggestions, such as: "When will Thérèse get a little brother?" or "You shouldn't put

---

* These were originally published in 2013 and 2014 in the online *Truth and Charity Forum*, which no longer exists.

too much space between your children, otherwise they can't play together anymore." I generally answer with a smile that we'd love to have more children, but that so far it hasn't worked out; in the meantime, the second comment has put a knife in my heart, not just making me feel sad once again for my husband and myself, but also for my daughter who will experience what it means to be an only child.

I know. I'm an only child myself. My parents also hoped to have many children but it didn't work out. I remember praying every day for a sibling until my teens. I didn't realize then that God answered my prayers in other ways: He gave me many cousins (over thirty) and He gave me some extraordinary friends who are like sisters to me, who are truly soulmates. But I would still have preferred for myself and for my daughter to have siblings.

People assume that only children are by definition spoiled, self-centered, and that sharing doesn't come easily to them. I have always found that unjust, and, like all prejudices, it makes one feel squeezed into a box. Especially as a child or teen, when one is more sensitive to how people react to or think of oneself, it makes one feel particularly powerless. What will it take for me to show you that I am none of the above? It's a losing battle.

Children can be spoiled by their parents whether they have siblings or not. Yes, it is more tempting to do so if parents have only one child. But the real spoiling happens through lack of guidance, lack of love, and letting children "get away" with selfish actions rather than correcting them and not just by giving them many things (though this can be a problem as well). I certainly had more toys (and unbroken ones at that) than my cousins; but my parents didn't let me get away with bad behavior of any kind, and I would have happily traded in those toys for the joy of playing with other children. It didn't take any toys for my cousins and me to come up with the best games to fill our hearts with joy and the house with laughter. And ironically, I often find myself having higher levels of tolerance when it comes to children's noise and mess than others who've had some siblings.

This is already a reassuring thought for parents with one child. There is no inbuilt deterministic fate which will make my only child become a selfish brat. Instead, it's a challenge for the child, requiring overcoming shyness and taking things into their hands. If they don't, then "only means lonely" (as a friend who is an only child herself once said to me). Rather than being spoiled, being a single child can be particularly challenging. One's parents can have particularly high expectations for their one and only. It means they can focus more on their child who cannot get away with anything (*"He* did it" doesn't work as an excuse for a single child). And they certainly don't want to fail with the one "project" they have in terms of childrearing.

On the positive end, parents have the opportunity of being particularly close to their child; there are no distractions. My mother took me along to a myriad of cultural events from the age of three (opera, museums, the ballet, etc.). I flourished, and it would have been hard to do this with a rambunctious crowd of children. The needs of the child are less likely to go unnoticed, while this is more prone to happen with many. There are many positives, though I'm not listing them to deny parents their need to mourn their lack of children (or make parents with many children feel bad).

Sometimes people experience the absence of children as a lack of God's blessing on them: "Children come from God, so if He doesn't give me any or more children, He must love me less." Or, "I wouldn't be as good of a parent as those with many children." But this is a twisted perception of God and has nothing to do with the infinite love He has for each one of us. Yes, children come from God, but God also bows down to our broken nature, affected by original sin, which has brought sickness and death into the world (and infertility is a form of illness).

Why does He sometimes work miracles while not in other cases? Why do some overcome infertility at least partially, while others remain childless? This remains a mystery and it takes much prayer to accept this cross with love; but one thing we can be sure of is that God does not love us less. His specific plans for each one of us, how they play out in our salvation and that of the world, will only be revealed in eternity. But for now, we can already know that He loves us infinitely and that He mourns our loss with us.

St. John the Baptist was an only child, the blessed Virgin as well, and some of the saints were only children. God has a special plan for each one of us. Therefore I need not feel terrible for my child who is missing out on siblings. Yes, it would be a richness to have more children. But one has no idea how the interaction between siblings would have been. We obviously can't know, but we at least shouldn't feel the burden that our child is missing out on something extraordinary.

Every child is infinitely precious, be they one of a crowd or alone. We need to welcome each child into the world in that spirit. Then we can fully enjoy those or the one we have.

WHEN MOTHER'S DAY
IS A DAY OF MOURNING:
SOME PASTORAL THOUGHTS

For many women, Mother's Day brings sadness. The infertile mourn the absence of children, others grieve the children they have lost through miscarriages, abortions, sickness, accidents, and wars. Others who had a difficult relationship with their mothers or who were perhaps abandoned or abused also have a hard time thinking of their mothers with gratitude. Those who have lost their mothers at a young age may grieve their absence. Women who never found a spouse and thus missed the joys of motherhood can find this day difficult as well.

Does this mean we should not celebrate Mother's Day? Of course not! However, there is a way of celebrating this day that pours salt into the wounds of those who are grieving. Unfortunately, I have found this to be very common. It is especially jarring when it happens during Mass. During the many years I was suffering from infertility, I tried to go to an early Mass on that day, hoping there would be no sermon. Or I would find myself torn between stoically gritting my teeth through it or discreetly leaving the church. Even once I had a child, the kinds of sermons I tended to hear still made me wince. Why? Because, for some reason, pastors on that day often speak in highly sentimental ways about motherhood.

Sentimentality is always in poor taste, though that is not my reason for taking umbrage with it here. The problem is that it falsifies reality. It makes one look at the world through a soppy lens from which the Cross is excluded. When suffering is mentioned, then it is only to be idealized and make one feel good about it somehow. The hero in second-rate, mushy literature, for example, might look all the more heroic for it, but his suffering has lost its sting to the reader. Though this may be a nice escape from reality (which explains its high selling rate in books, music, and movies) which one might indulge in now and then, it has no place in a homily—not only because the priest is not supposed to conjure up a world without suffering which we can no longer find here since the Garden of Eden, but also because it is pastorally poisonous, especially for those who are suffering. The grieving are confronted with an unrealistic ideal, making them feel all the more lonely in their sorrow, being shut out from it.

But doesn't this kind of logic mean we cannot talk about anything anymore, given that every topic will in some shape or form be painful for someone out there? Wouldn't this mean never speaking about the Holy Family, given that some, perhaps many in the congregation, have been raised in abusive and dysfunctional families? This is a completely different case. The Holy Family did not live in a sentimental world, nor did they romanticize their surroundings. We might be tempted to sentimentalize the stable since we bracket out the rejection preceding it as well as the poverty and difficulties surrounding Christ's birth. Mary and Joseph were turned away in Bethlehem and then were persecuted by Herod, who massacred the Holy Innocents in Bethlehem while the Holy Family fled to Egypt. Theirs was not an easy life, and its earthly culmination ended on Golgotha. Even the Resurrection does not do away with the Cross—but a sentimental world does.

Those who come to church with a heart full of grief can find solace in God's love, in the examples of the Blessed Mother and all the saints. They too went through this valley of tears and the way their trials brought them closer to God can therefore be a consolation to others. God Himself became flesh to share our sufferings; no one can therefore be closer to us in our sorrows than Him. Through the examples of Christ and the saints, we can experience a kind of love we missed and discover that we can carry our crosses with peace in our hearts, even if they remain painful. A sentimental lie, however, cannot bring any authentic comfort, and if it gives some relief through escapism, then it will only be of short duration.

Rather than trying to make us feel gratitude toward our mothers and those who have been like mothers to us by a clichéd depiction of motherhood, the sermon on that day should focus on a different kind of maternity. No matter what we have suffered as children and as mothers, as singles and as childless women, Mary is a mother to all of us. She went through the greatest suffering imaginable, seeing her son mocked, despised, and die a horrific death on the Cross. Her suffering can resonate with those suffering as mothers or simply from broken hearts. Hers is a kind of motherhood which is timeless, for it is not limited by class, background, or culture. The Virgin Mary was humble and poor. Her life can therefore speak to all, since we are all broken and wounded. Of course, one can also sentimentalize her. No topic or model is immune to being romanticized if one is sufficiently bent on doing so. But by focusing on her or other saints, one is less likely to fall into the trap of sentimentality.

Saints like St. Gianna Beretta Molla or Chiara Corbella speak to those who are suffering as mothers, for their motherhood became their Calvary.[1] They heroically gave their lives for their

---

[1] See my articles on the topic: Marie Meaney, "Chiara Corbella: A Witness to Joy," *Crisis Magazine*, April 16, 2014, http://www.crisismagazine.com/20 14/chiara-corbella-a-witness-to-joy; Marie Meaney, "The Gift of Joy," The Personalist Project, April 22, 2014, http://www.thepersonalistproject.org /comments/the_gift_of_joy.

children, while leaving a beloved husband and child(ren) behind. Their stories transcend their time and culture, thus speaking to many people. Through their examples, one can grasp what motherhood is really about and why all women are called to it, whether they are single or married, childless or the mother of many. Motherhood is about the gift of self to which everyone is called. For most, this does not express itself in such an obviously heroic fashion. But if lived fully, it changes the everyday and turns the daily difficulties and sacrifices into expressions of this gift of self, which can be just as radical as that of Gianna or Chiara.

By showing their congregations that a radical gift of self is at the heart of motherhood, priests are more likely to arouse in the hearts of their parishioners real gratitude toward their mothers. Sentimentality is a brief, passing feeling; it is easily kindled and falls to ashes just as easily. There is no real love behind it. Schmaltziness will not make me assist my mother through her declining years and painful sicknesses. But desiring to respond to her self-giving love by the same kind of love will. And if she failed to love me, then God's love can inspire me to help her nonetheless. Through suffering, our hearts can be purified from their selfishness; real love can arise out of it. However, by denying the necessity of embracing the Cross, sentimentality eliminates the very medicine we need to cure us from our hardness of heart. Ultimately, it is opposed to real love, just as it is opposed to authentic art.

Let us not cheapen the Church's rich currents of spirituality by sprinkling sentimentality on them. This syrupy sweetness will undermine their transforming force. It is tempting to deny the Cross by romanticizing it, but that won't do us any good. The suffering need real food to nourish their souls, not marshmallow spirituality which will make them sick. Not a Hallmark, feel-good worldview, but Christ's Cross and Resurrection are the answer.

Hence Mother's Day is the occasion to speak about the sword which pierces women's hearts—about the Cross which we must all embrace so that it becomes a tree of life. Only radical love—the kind where one gives until it hurts—will do, while sentimentality will at best be a Band-Aid covering a festering wound.

WANTING ONE MORE: DEALING WITH
SECONDARY INFERTILITY

After nine years of marriage, our little Thérèse Marie arrived on the feast day of the archangels in 2009. Great was our joy after all these years of waiting, longing, mourning, hoping, and doubting that this would ever happen. We finally held our little daughter in our arms after thirty-three hours of labor ending in a C-section. I came to experience what so many mothers had told me about: the deep happiness of having a child making you forget the pains of labor and yearning to go through them all over again to have more children. Our happiness seemed complete—as much as it can be this side of the grave—and the doctors gave us the hope that with the birth of one child more children might be forthcoming. I felt the pangs of longing almost immediately, and each time I drove by the hospital, I hoped I might be returning there again soon for another delivery.

Women suffering from secondary infertility had told me about the pain which comes from having less children than one wants.[1] I even met one woman who was distraught since she had hoped for a ninth child who, now that she had had a hysterectomy in her mid-forties, would never be born. I tried to empathize. The pain seemed real, but I wasn't quite prepared for what was to come. Don't get me wrong. It makes a universe of difference to have one child rather than none. The joy of parenting is there, day after day, in discovering the world anew through one's child's eyes and

---

[1] Secondary infertility is generally defined as not being able to conceive or carry a pregnancy to term within twelve months (if one is under thirty-five) or within six months (if one is thirty-five or over) after one's cycle has started again.

feeling their love in so many ways. One's life has changed its focus and is centered on the growth and well-being of this little one.

But when the longing grows very strong again, one looks at one's medical options, wonders which therapies one should try this time, and is sad at the thought that one's child might not have any siblings or less than one would want. I've written about the pain which comes from lack of empathy concerning infertility; it is just as real with secondary infertility. Infertile couples tend to get less understanding, since people are under the impression that they are now "healed" and that they should be perfectly happy since they finally have a child. It can be unnerving to have witnessed the pain of infertility in a couple for many years and now that they have a child and should be joyful (so one thinks) to see that they are still suffering. This seems to border on ingratitude or indicates a negative outlook on life—at least that's the feedback infertile couples can get. But one can be very happy about having a child or children and yet mourn deeply that one doesn't have more. Obviously, the sufferings are very different for the couple who is blessed with an abundant fertility. They too may be very glad about each one of their children and yet feel crushed by fatigue and worries.

In both cases joy and suffering can go hand in hand, and it takes Christian charity to empathize with each other—the fertile and the infertile—in situations which are polar opposites. Making it difficult to bear the other's complaints—and it is good to be aware of this—can be one's own unacknowledged suffering. One might ask oneself, "How can that other person complain about too few children when I am dead tired because my children don't allow me to sleep?" Or, "I am in deep pain since I haven't been given the gift of abundant fertility." The problem lies not so much with the other person expressing their suffering but with the fact that my pain hasn't been heard, that I've perhaps been stoic about it. It's a reminder that we often do not know each other's hidden crosses, and that we may well drive another nail in without knowing it.

If one's history of infertility includes miscarriages, the pain is very intense. Most women suffer acutely from their miscarriages, no matter what their story is. If they longed for children for an extended period, then a miscarriage breaks open the pain of their infertility in a new way. It feels like a nasty trick: they are given a child briefly only to have it snatched away before they've even held them in their arms. It often takes much grieving under the Cross to be able to accept this loss and not blame God. Even though it is a consolation to know we will meet our children in heaven, this does not do away with the grief of missing this child here and now. This hope should not be used in an attempt to shorten the grieving process either by oneself or by others.

There seems no adequate human answer for our deep woundedness and pain, no real consolation. The only person capable of responding fully to this seemingly infinite pain is Christ: He wants to be invited into our grief and sin. He alone, being the Truth, can fully see and acknowledge our suffering and help us bear it instead of adding further pain through denial and lack of compassion. Only if we carry our cross with Him are we free to experience joy and fully empathize with another's pain without being distracted by our own. And only if we are transformed sufficiently by Him are we able to stand with others under the Cross and be of true comfort.

WHAT IVF AND EUTHANASIA
HAVE IN COMMON

In vitro fertilization (IVF) and euthanasia seem strange bedfellows. "Polar opposites" is what comes to mind at first. After all, the one is about generating new life, it would seem, while the other is about ending it prematurely. Yet after hearing about two cases of IVF among my acquaintances recently, I was struck by the fact that they have more in common than we think and that the mentality behind the one leads to the other.

A mother at my daughter's preschool told me about her IVF procedure. She had lied to her doctor about the length of time she and her husband had tried to conceive—it had been eight months instead of twelve. For some reason, she was convinced they would never have children naturally, panicked (she was in her late thirties), and decided to take the IVF route as quickly as possible.

Even if one has no ethical or other issues with *in vitro*, this woman's story—as I heard more—told me that this had been an unnecessary procedure. She'd had a miscarriage less than a year before attempting IVF which shows that she was able to conceive. Had she been truthful and confided in her doctor, she might have found out that this miscarriage was in a certain respect promising, that she would probably have conceived again and have been able to carry to term the next pregnancy. This was confirmed by the sequel to the story: Two years after her IVF-conceived child was born, she prepared for another *in vitro* fertilization. However, a few days before they started with the procedure, she found out she had gotten pregnant naturally.

That IVF is often unnecessary and that other procedures such as the Creighton method of natural family planning and

NaProTechnology are statistically much more successful than IVF is generally unknown, as is the fact that *in vitro* is fraught with many potential medical and psychological problems—not to speak of the moral issues. But this is not what I want to focus on here. What strikes me in this case (as well as in another one I heard of recently where the couple, though attempting to conceive naturally for a year, didn't try much else and immediately turned to IVF) is the lack of patience and the need for complete control these couples exhibited.

I have much sympathy for infertile couples and their sufferings since it took us nine years before we had a little daughter, and we've been suffering from secondary infertility for some years now. It is particularly difficult to feel utterly out of control, to be waiting month after month, have one's hopes go up only to see them dashed yet again. There are still so many unknowns regarding infertility that doctors can't pinpoint what the problem is in about 20% of the cases or vary in their predictions as to the likelihood of a given couple having children (doctors have told me everything from we would never have children to prophesying with much conviction that we would). It feels like one is banging one's head against a wall, and there seems little one can do to fulfill one's desire for a child if one's condition doesn't happen to be easily detectable and treatable. IVF therefore seems to many the much longed-for solution to cut short this painful waiting. That IVF only has a 30% success rate during the first cycle (which includes three rounds of attempted implantation), that many women miscarry, and the physical and psychological risks for the child, mother, and egg donors often remain undisclosed.[1] Many

---

[1] "IVF Linked to Intellectual Disability, Autism in Children: Large Study," *LifeSiteNews*, July 19, 2013, http://www.lifesitenews.com/news/ivf-linked

infertile couples would rather attempt something with a low success rate than nothing at all.

Patience comes from the Latin word *pati* which means to suffer; thus, patience is required by and is at the very core of suffering. Bearing a chronic illness, a slow decline, or a condition which one can't resolve or control is particularly difficult. One is being stretched to one's limits, at least that's the way it feels—only to be stretched even further, having to bear the unbearable. It is only natural to seek a way out and one should do so, as long as the solution doesn't go against the dignity of the human person and thus make us commit morally wrong acts.

Suffering is a trial which either teaches patience or leads to rebellion and despair. Our age seems particularly in want of the first. Everything is fast paced. We've lost the sense that good things are worth waiting for, while some things have to be borne, and that there is some meaning to be found in and personal growth which can come from suffering. We want immediate gratification, and hence lost time (or what feels like it), suffering, and lack of control become inacceptable. It is a terrible thing to be stripped of one's heart's desire, of health, of happiness. It becomes unacceptable when all one has to look forward to is the here and now. If this is the only life I have, then having no children, no spouse, no success, no riches is to be avoided at all cost, as is suffering in general.

That cost, as it turns out, can be life itself. It is the lives of the *in vitro* children that are discarded since they are less than perfect or who are frozen and abandoned. The life of my wanted IVF child is built on the grave of their siblings. Those who demand euthanasia in order to avoid a long and painful dying process put

---

-to-intellectual-disability-autism-in-children-large-study; Adams, "IVF 'Could Double Risk of Cerebral Palsy.'"

not only themselves at risk (for it may turn out that they are quite willing to live on, after all) but those others who don't have a say. Children will soon be legally euthanized in Belgium. People who are disabled, comatose, or seriously ill have been killed for many years under the radar screen, without drawing the attention of the media or having their family put up a fight. It has mainly been a silent killing so far; now it is coming out into the open.

IVF and euthanasia promise the avoidance of suffering, but this proves to be a lie. Suffering should not be avoided at all costs; otherwise, it comes back to haunt us in other, worse ways. I personally know some families where a member demanded to be legally euthanized for fear of old age and sickness. These families are left distraught and troubled, feeling abandoned by their loved one who didn't trust them sufficiently to walk this difficult path with them. There is no act—let alone an act of such magnitude—without an impact on others and society at large. People conceived through IVF speak of the trauma they have experienced despite the love of their parents. Some feel violated by having been conceived in a cold lab rather than through the intimate embrace of their parents, and feel instrumentalized in order to cater to the needs of their parents. Either I am willing to carry my cross with the grace of God and the help of others, or I will throw it on other people's shoulders.

The Cross is tremendously heavy if we carry it on our own. Christ promises that it will become light if we carry it with Him. It becomes unbearable if we try to discard it. If we do, then the consequences of our acts will come to haunt us for generations to come like the Furies in Greek tragedy. The choice is ours to make.

RESOURCES

www.hannahstears.org

Hannah's Tears offers spiritual support for the brokenhearted who suffer from infertility, miscarriage, stillbirth, or the loss of a child at any age. The people involved in this ministry help each other by sharing each other's crosses, following the example of Simon of Cyrene.

www.popaulvi.com

The Pope Paul VI Institute for the Study of Human Reproduction in Omaha, Nebraska was founded by Dr. Thomas Hilgers and his wife Sue in 1985. It is a multi-faceted organization which dedicates its programs of research, education, ethics, and service to building strong marriages and healthy families. As the Institute pursues the development of a morally and professionally acceptable reproductive health service, it is committed to the development of a culture of life based on responsible parenthood, responsible fertility regulation, and ethical means for the treatment of infertility and related reproductive disorders.

www.naprotechnology.com

The Pope Paul VI Institute promotes the Creighton Model FertilityCare System (CrMS), an advanced natural family planning system which links gynecological and procreative healthcare and health maintenance. Their fertility care system is called NaProTechnology (Natural Procreative Technology), a new women's health science that monitors and maintains a woman's reproductive and gynecological health. It provides medical and surgical treatments that cooperate completely with the reproductive system.

www.aafcp.org

The American Academy of Fertility Care Professionals (AAFCP) is another resource to find pro-life fertility care help. They address all sides of infertility including the emotional aspect (www.aafcp .org/emotional_aspects.html).

www.boma-usa.org

The Billings Ovulation Method is a method of natural family planning based on the observation of the woman's cervical mucus and was developed by Drs. John and Evelyn Billings. It is less complicated than the Creighton Model FertilityCare System and is therefore a good way to start monitoring one's fertility.

www.omsoul.com

One More Soul is a global supplier of educational resources fostering God's plan for love, marriage, and procreation.

www.ncbcenter.org

The National Catholic Bioethics Center in Philadelphia gives individual bioethical consults for free.